Anonymous

Evidence Taken Before the Committee of the House of
Representatives,

Appointed to Enquire Into the Treatment of Prisoners at Castle Thunder

Anonymous

Evidence Taken Before the Committee of the House of Representatives,
Appointed to Enquire Into the Treatment of Prisoners at Castle Thunder

ISBN/EAN: 9783337148539

Printed in Europe, USA, Canada, Australia, Japan

Cover: Foto ©ninafisch / pixelio.de

More available books at **www.hansebooks.com**

EVIDENCE

TAKEN BEFORE THE

COMMITTEE OF THE HOUSE OF REPRESENTATIVES,

APPOINTED TO ENQUIRE INTO THE TREATMENT OF PRISONERS AT CASTLE THUNDER.

Saturday, April 11th, 1863.

WILLIAM CAUSEY, sworn.—I live in Elizabeth City county; but have been in Richmond since January, 1861, employed as a detective in General Winder's detective police force.

I know something of the treatment of the prisoners. They are put in huddles, sometimes five hundred and seven hundred in one building. Sometimes they are treated well by the commandant and the wardens; but I have seen them severely punished. I have seen them tied by the thumbs, and raised up on their toes. I don't think their's could have been very aggravted offences; rather think it was for disagreements among themselves. I don't know how long they remained tied up, but, from the best information, they were kept sometimes eight hours. I don't know that any of the sick prisoners were thus treated. I saw a man hand-cuffed around a post, raised up at first and afterwards cut down when his blood had stagnated. I don't know what offence he had committed. On another occasion a canteen of gun-powder was exploded in the prison room by some of the prisoners. The powder was collected from cartridges, and was not much in quantity. I heard the report of it ten minutes after its occurrence, and rode up to General Winder's office with Captain Alexander. While in General Winder's office Captain Alexander reported the circumstances of the powder explosion. I don't know what the General said, but Captain Alexander went back to the prison, and put the men down in the pen outside, where they remained two or three days. They had no covering, and it was raining. The men in the pen were those in the room where the powder was exploded. Captain Alexander demanded the names of those who put the powder in the stove, and because the men refused to tell, put them all in the pen. It was last fall, in the month of November, I think. I heard of some of them dying shortly afterwards. They died after that I am positive, but I never knew their names. Prisoners guilty of bad offences have irons on them generally, but I don't think any of the men put in the pen had irons on.

I think two men have been shot at the prison since Captain Alexander has been in charge, and one on Franklin street at the guard-house. The man killed at the guard-house was shot while attempting to escape. In my opinion, all could have been arrested without being shot. The desperate men were generally put in Castle Godwin. The soldiers picked up on the street are put in this prison. Castle Godwin is not part of Castle Thunder; Thunder was Godwin's successor in cognomen after removal. The man shot a few nights ago at Castle Thunder certainly could have been captured without shooting. There is a standing order to shoot only if he cannot otherwise be arrested.

I have seen prisoners whipped; but I don't know by whose or what authority. I have seen men severely whipped on the buttocks with straps; don't know how many lashes were laid on, but I should think about fifty. I only saw one whipping. On this occasion the officers were requested by Captain Alexander to go up into the prison room and see the men whipped. The whipping strap was secured on to wooden handles. They were made of harness leather or sole leather from eighteen inches to two feet in length. The blows were laid on about as hard as a man could do it. I have seen prisoners wear the same clothes for months until they were ready to drop off in rags. I think there have been instances of attempts to bribe the guard.

Schaffer, sworn.—I reside in Richmond, and am a detective in General Winder's force. The prisoners are treated according to their behavior. Some of them, I think, I have been cruelly treated. They were punished sometimes for fighting, sometimes for stealing. I have seen them whipped, one received fifteen lasshes, another twenty-five, and a third fifty lashes. The prisoner that received fifty lashes was pretty severely cut.

I know something about putting the prisoners out in the back yard. It was in November, and it was raining during a portion of the time. They were put there for exploding gunpowder in the building. The prisoners who were put out were put there because they would not tell who did it. Some of those men died afterwards. I could not say who gave the order to put the men in the yard, but I suppose Captain Alexander ordered them to be put there. They had generally wollen clothes on. Two men have been killed in Castle Thunder, and one in Franklin street guard house. The man last mentioned was attempting to escape when shot. Of the other men, one of them was a deranged man, and was put in a cell. He got out of the cell, and in attempting to get away was halted by the sentinel, but not heeding, was shot by him. He was a Yankee prisoner, brought from the Libby prison, and shot the same night. I have seen two men whipped in Castle Thunder, but it was done by order of the court martial.

I have seen prisoners "bucked" for one or two hours. Some of them had attempted to escape ; others had been insulting to the officers of the prison. Some of the prisoners are well clad, and others very poorly. Some have no bed clothing. I have been connected with the prison over one year. I know the prisoners need clothing, and common decency requires that they should be better clothed. The prison is kept very clean, as clean as it well can be. The printed rules require this. I have never heard the officers of the prison abuse the prisoners unless the prisoners were refractory. One prisoners' clotning is very frequently stolen by the others.

Robert B. Crow sworn.—I am a resident of Richmond, and have been for forty years. I am one of the detective force under the Provost Marshal, or rather, General Winder. Of the treatment of the prisoners at Castle Thunder, I know very little except from hearsay, as my position does not require me beyond the office. I can recall an instance or two of their treatment. On one occasion, I remember, Captain Alexander had one of the prisoners whipped for garroting or robbing another prisoner, I did not see him whipped, but heard that he was whipped, and I presume the captain gave the order to have him whipped. I do not know whether he was whipped on his bare back or not. I say I do not know it of my own knowledge, but I think he was. I know of the prisoners being turned out in the Castle yard, but do not know what their offence was. It was in quite cold weather, and rainy, and they had nothing to cover them but the clothing they had on, and no roof covering to shelter them. I do not know what their offence was ; do not know what rations they had while out there, nor whether they had bed clothing or not. The yard is an ordinary one, walled in ; do not know how large it is. I know two or three prisoners to have been ki'led at the Castle. One was the case of a Yankee who was shot, and the other case that of the deserter, (Carroll,) shot the other night in trying to escape. The one that was shot last was shot lying down, dragging himself along the balcony, trying to get out. I was not present at the time. Some of the prisoners are well clad, and others again are very indifferently clothed. The prison room is comfortable ; there is a very large stove in it.

T. G. Bland sworn.—I am from Louisiana, and was former steward of the prison hospital. I went there on the 10th of November last, and was relieved from duty on the 4th of the present month. In regard to the treatment of the prisoners confined there, I myself was a prisoner four months in Fort Delaware. and, from experience, I consider the prisoners treated well there to what they are here. I consider them most barbarously and inhumanely treated. On one occasion ten or fifteen of the prisoners were brought out in a large hall, two of them accused of stealing from the prisoners. Two out:

of the number brought out were not whipped, they were sick, I believe, and that was the reason. I do not think the whipping was done by order of the court martial, as Captain Alexander had the men brought out himself. The prisoners were stripped and whipped on the bare back, each receiving ten or twelve lashes laid on by the strongest man in Captain Bossieux's company. The words Captain Alexander used while the whipping was going on were "lay it on!" They were whipped for stealing money, and, as they were all hard cases, every one of them, some of them did steal it, no doubt, but none had a chance of vindicating themselves. They were tied up to a post and whipped. The general treatment of the prisoners is very good, but some of the officers of the prison treat the prisoners as though they were dogs instead of soldiers, fighting in the common cause of the Confederacy.

[Captain Alexander here suggested that the witnesses be kept separate from the witness delivering his testimony, as customary in proceedings of the kind before the committee. The Chairman of the committee said he judged the witnesses present were all honorable men, and would not suffer their own ideas to be influenced by the testimony of a witness. He, however, yielded the point, and all the witnesses except the one under investigation were sent from the committee room.]

Mr. BLAND resumed.—I have heard of men being killed at the prison. I helped to put one in a coffin myself, and sent the corpse to the undertaker. He was shot while trying to escape. I have seen men handcuffed around a large pillow, and one of these I saw so punished was taken from the hospital. His offence was trying to bribe the guard. Neither had irons on them. The sick man was under the surgeon's care then. He was handcuffed around the pillow between five and six o'clock in the afternoon, and when I got back to the prison at eleven o'clock the same night, he was still there, and I do not know how long after that. The worst characters in the prison are handcuffed, and wear ball and chain; the others, who are not so desperate, are left to go free. Those tied up could not have been in for very serious offences. I know the prisoners were put out in the yard, and kept there for two or three days. Some of them were thinly and badly clothed, and others were well clad. The citizen prisoners are generally clothed well, and the soldiers poorly, having no change. Some of those exposed in the yard were brought up into the hospital afterwards, sick with the pneumonia, and I heard the surgeon (Dr. Coggin) say that the exposure in the yard made them ill, and nothing else. Several of them died in the hospital of pneumonia. The season was in November, with cold, rainy weather. I know of one direct violation of the army regulations of the Confederate States, and that was in regard to treatment received by myself. It was for disobeying an order of Captain Alexander. The order was to prescribe for a patient. I am not a graduated physician, and it was against the orders of the surgeon in charge. I was ordered to a dungeon in which I could not stand up straight, a cell about six feet square. I had no chance to vindicate myself, as I sent for Captain Alexander and he did not visit me. I was kept in the dungeon until the next morning. I have known prisoners to be kept there three or four days. I have seen, on one or two occasions, fifteen or twenty prisoners "bucked" and "gagged" at a time. The "gag" is effected by a stick inserted crosswise in the mouth, and the "buck" is to tie the arms at the elbows to a cross piece beneath the thighs. They were generally ironed, wore ball and chain, and were charged with various offences. I recollect now I only "gagged" one. I have seen the "barrel shirt" worn by a prisoner. The shirt is made by sawing a common flour barrel in twain, and cutting arm holes in the sides, and an aperture in the barrel head for the insertion of the wearer's head. The one I saw have the barrel shirt on wore it as a punishment for fighting. He was tied up by the thumbs to the roof, and stood on his feet, wearing it one day and part of the next day. Do not know how much longer he wore it.

JOHN CAPHART sworn.—I have been employed with Captain Alexander eleven months, on the detective force; seven months of that time I have been at the prison. I have never seen a prisoner harshly treated except by orders. It was realy dangerous at times for the officers to go among the prisoners, some of them were such desperate characters. A new prisoner sent in among them was usually knocked down, beat and robbed, if he had anything about him. I was off and on duty at the prison, sleeping there. One night I would be off duty and go to my room at eight o'clock, and another night at ten o'clock. I remember the occasion of the difficulty between Captain Alexander and Mr. Bland. The captain gave him an order to render service to a sick child. Bland refused to obey, and Captain Alexander again reiterated his order and Bland again refused with an oath. I then put him in the cell, by the the order of Captain Alexander. Bland was intoxicated on that occasion. I have seen men whipped at the prison, by order of the court martial and General Winder, and by order of Captain Alexander, through General Winder, (by the latter generally) for stealing from prisoners and the mal-treatment of prisoners. I have seen prisoners tied up by the arms. They were two men whom nobody could manage. They were not tied up by the thumbs. The whipping was all done with a leather thong or strap, about two feet long. In regard to the barrel shirt, I saw one of Captain Bossieux's men walking in one, by order of the court martial.

———

Monday, April 13, 1863.

The examination of witnesses was resumed. JOHN CAPHART, detective, was recalled to the stand.

Question by Captain Alexander.—Mr. Caphart, how many years of your life were you connected with prisons before you came with me?

Answer.—Thirty-one years, sir.

Question.—How does my treatment of prisoners compare with what you have seen in other prisons?

Answer.—Very favorable. For offences such as have been committed in the Castle by the prisoners, they would be put in irons. As I said before, at one time it was dangerous to go into the prison room. It was necessary to observe great caution in going in among them. I did not feel safe unless I went with one hand on my pistol.

Question.—Do you think you ever saw a worse set in any jail.

Answer.—No I never did; They would be ironed down to ring-bolts in the floor, for conduct such as I have seen at the Castle.

Question.—They chain men down in jails then, do they?

Answer.—Yes, I have seen it done, and helped to do it.

Question.—You have been eleven months with me as commandant of Castle Thunder post. What is my manner and demeanor towards the prisoners?

Answer.—Usually kind on all occasions. Men reported to you for misconduct you have sometimes imprisoned them.

Question.—Have you not seen persons who came to the Castle, spit upon by the prisoners from the windows, and the sentinels cursed and abused?

Answer.—Yes, I have seen it done many times.

Question.—When prisoners are brought in under arrest and I am present, do I not attempt to discriminate, and instruct the officers to separate and classify them, and assign them different quarters according to their appearance or offence?

Answer.—Yes, I have seen it done and know it was done.

Question.—Do you know anything of the plot gotten up among the prisoners to assassinate me and other officers, set the board yard on fire, and liberate the prisoners?

Answer.—Yes, I heard of it, and it is a well established fact, and A. C. Webster, who was hanged, was the ringleader of the plot.

Question.—And all this when Webster was afterwards condemned to death; what was my conduct towards him?

Answer.—You cut and fixed his food, and set up with him after he received his injuries in attempting to escape.

Question by Mr. Ward, counsel for Captain Alexander.—Mr. Caphart, will you tell the committee how James Tyree was treated by the prisoners when first put into the Castle?

Answer.—Yes; I remember when Tyree was brought to the prison, he was dressed in a suit of black and looked genteel and nice. He was sent up stairs and put in one of the rooms. In a few minutes I heard a tremendous noise of shouting, yelling and hallooing, mingled with cries. I went up as fast as I could, and found Tyree all beaten and gory with blood, and stripped to his drawers. He was so bloody and bruised that I could hardly recognize him. I rescued him and took him out from among the prisoners, and they followed and crowded around, yelling "let me at him once more, the son of a bitch; kill the son of a bitch, &c." I carried him outside of the railing and the prisoners attempted to come over the railing after him. Tyree had nothing but his drawers on then. The clothing was never found.

Question by the Committee.—How many more cases of· this kind do you know about?

Answer.—I know of one case, an old man, fifty years old, who was beaten and died from the effects of it.

CAPTAIN ALEXANDER.—That was a case of murder outright.

Question by Mr. Ward.—Did you ever see more lenient treatment by the captain of such incorrigable prisoners?

Answer.—Never in my life, sir. Never saw prisoners better treated. Such misbehavior elsewhere would have led to their close confinement.

By the Chairman of the Committee.—You say the prisoners are dangerous to each other and visitors?

Answer.—Not now, sir, since the whipping.

Question.—How many do the guard number?

Answer.—Fourteen, or about that number.

Question.—Did you ever know visitors to the prison to be attacked?

Answer.—Yes, sir. Always told visitors to look out when they went where the prisoners were. I have seen beef bones large enough to knock a man down thrown at visitors. Once the commandant and all of his officers had to retreat from a shower of beef bones.

Question.—How long since were the prisoners so desperate?

Answer.—Before the whipping of the ringleaders. The conduct of the prisoners have improved since.

Question.—Were some of the men whipped brought from the room from whence ·he beef bones were hurled?

Answer.—Yes, sir.

Question.—What for?

Answer.—For fighting, stealing, and other offences.

Question.—How did you know they were the men?

Answer.—They were pointed out by the other prisoners. The captain said he would have them all whipped unless they pointed out the guilty ones. They did so, and the guilty ones stepped out.

Question.—How many men were brought out to be whipped?

Answer.—I think there were eight or ten.

Question.—Were these men whipped for fighting?

Answer.—Yes, sir, they were.

Question.—How do you know they were the right men?

Answer.—I do not know for certain whether the men whipped were the right ones or not, but the other prisoners said so. They were engaged among others, and were pointed out by the other prisoners.

Question.—How many prisoners were beaten in that fracas?

Answer.—Several. One old man named Mitchell was beaten so dreadfully that he has been crazy ever since.

Question.—Do you know the provocation for the fight, and was it enquired into?

Answer.—I know of no provocation. The case was enquired into by Captain Alexander. There was a great change after the whipping. All was quiet and we could go in and out without molestation.

Question.—How many rooms are there in the prison?

Answer.—In the second story there is a large hall, and beyond that a large sized room where citizens and disloyal persons are confined, and on the third story is a very large room for the soldiers, and partitioned cells, or rather rooms, for prisoners tried by court martial, and prisoners awaiting trial by court martial.

Captain Alexander to Committee.—We get so accustomed to the men received at Castle Thunder, that we know their character as soon as they come in, and are thus guided in our disposition of them.

Mr. Ward, counsel to Committee.—Men are often received from the commanding officer of a company, accompanied by an order running something like this : " Take this man and put him in a cell, and feed him on bread and water till I send for him, for he is one of the damndest rascals in the world."

Captain Alexander.—Such irresponsible orders are never observed nor followed out, though.

Question by Committee—Was the whipping referred to, by order of General Winder ?

Answer.—Yes, sir, it was. I carried the order myself from the general to the captain.

WILLIAM CAUSEY, detective, was recalled to the stand.

Question by Committee.—Do you know anything about prisoners who were whipped, and if so, whether they were Confederate volunteers ?

Answer.—Yes, sir, and I think they were volunteer soldiers, for there are no others there.

Question.—Do you know what was their crime ?

Answer.—No, sir.

Question.—Did not you hear something about a row among the prisoners ?

Answer.—No, sir, I only saw some men whipped.

Question.—How long have you been a detective ?

Answer.—Since March last twelve months ago. I left the Castle six or eight days ago, and was transferred to the provost marshal's office.

Question.—Up to the time you left, were the prisoners there all Confederate volunteers ?

Answer.—Yes, sir.

Question.—Were there any Yankee prisoners there ?

Answer.—Yes ; there were some in the lower room, sent from the Libby prison when it was full.

Question.—What is Caphart's character as an officer ?

Answer.—I should say he was rather rough.

Question.—In his general deportment towards the prisoners is he humane or otherwise ?

Answer.—He was otherwise, I should think. He would curse them, shake his stick, and talk of how he would serve them.

Question.—From the tenor of his remarks, would you suppose he would be gratified rather than humiliated at the chastisement of a soldier ?

Answer.—Rather gratified, I think.

By Mr. Ward.—Causey, don't you think Caphart a good officer and detective?

Answer.—I do not, sir.

Question.—Did you ever hear Caphart exult over a man whom he thought was punished properly or justly?

Answer.—I don't know his thoughts; I can't answer that question.

Question.—From his conversation did you think he thought the men were justly punished?

Answer.—No, sir, I did not.

Question.—Did you ever hear him express any regrets that they were whipped?

Answer.—No, sir.

Question by Captain Alexander.—Do you know whether the prisoners whipped were Yankees or Confederate volunteers?

Answer.—I think they were Confederate volunteers.

Question by Mr. Ward.—Have you been in the habit of visiting the prisoners?

Answer.—Rarely or never, except on business.

Question.—Did you see the men whipped?

Answer.—I did.

Question by Captain Alexander.—How many lashes were given them, and did you hear the sentence of the court martial?

Answer.—I think it was by order of the court martial.

Question.—Where was the whipping done?

Answer.—Up stairs.

Question.—On what part of the body was the lash laid on?

Answer.—On the *buttocks*, I think.

Question.—Did you see any prisoners tied up?

Answer.—Yes; lifted up on their toes.

Question.—Did you ever knock a prisoner down?

Answer.—No, sir.

Question.—Did you ever strike a prisoner?

Answer.—Yes, after the prisoner struck me.

Question by Chairman of Committee.—What is Captain Alexander's treatment of the prisoners generally?

Answer.—He is sometimes kind, and sometimes the reverse of kindness.

Question by Mr. Ward.—Do you know what provocation the Captain had in thus speaking?

Answer.—No. But I have heard him speak very snappish when prisoners were being put in. He expressed himself only in language.

Question.—What was his language?

Answer.—Well, something like "shove them in there." "Put them in there, God damn them."

Question by Mr Ward.—Did not the prisoners refuse to be put back sometimes, and resist, so much so as to require the exercise of force?

Answer.—I never had a prisoner to refuse to go in; but I have had them to resist me on the street.

J. F. Schaffer, detective, was recalled to the stand.

Question by Chairman of Committee.—What is the deportment of Caphart towards prisoners?

Answer.—I have known him to be very abusive, generally when prisoners were impudent to him. I have heard him curse prisoners under arrest, when they held back or resisted him.

Question.—Did you ever see men tied up by the thumbs?

Answer.—I have seen prisoners tied up either by the thumbs or the wrists. It is called "trysting up," and is a sailor's punishment.

Question by Mr. Ward.—Did you ever examine to see by which they were tied, the thumbs or the wrists?

Answer.—No, sir.

Question by Chairman of Committee.—For what offences were those you saw tied up?

Answer.—For bribing the guard, I believe. I don't know whether they were Yankees or Confederate volunteers.

Question.—Do you remember, on a certain occasion, when eight or ten men were whipped?

Answer.—I heard it rumored; did'nt see it.

Question.—Is Caphart's conduct towards prisoners abusive?

Answer.—No, except on occasions; he was rather kind.

Question by Mr. Ward.—Mr. Schaffer, don't you think Caphart as good an officer as there is on the force?

Answer.—I must say I have heard him abuse the prisoners very much. I have heard him use some very harsh language towards them.

Question by Captain Alexander.—Who is the most passionate of the two, Causey or Caphart?

Answer.—I couldn't say.

Question by Chairman of Committee.—Is Caphart kind and humane towards the prisoners, or the reverse?

Answer.—I cannot say.

By Captain Alexander.—You know him to be a kind husband and father, don't you?

Answer.—I never saw him in the midst of his family; so I cannot say.

Robert B. Crow, detective, was recalled to the stand.

Question by Chairman.—You know Caphart?

Answer.—Yes, sir, I do.

Question.—What is his general disposition; is he kind?

Answer.—He is exactly the reverse of that?

Question.—Did you ever hear him express any regrets for punishment inflicted upon soldiers?

Answer.—No, sir; he rather exulted at it. . I have heard him say "damn them, I'd take a knife and cut them in pieces."

Question.—Does he treat them roughly or kindly?

Answer.—Very roughly indeed.

Question.—Without provocation?

Answer.—He is generally rough; it is natural with him. I have seen him shove and push prisoners about as though they were negroes.

I never heard him express any regrets, but rather exulted at their treatment.

Question.—How many prisoners are usually confined in the Castle?

Answer.—Between 400 and 500; sometimes more, and sometimes less. They are constantly being received and discharged.

Question.—How often is it found necessary to punish the prisoners?

Answer.—I don't know. I seldom go up among the prisoners. I have seen whippings inflicted three or four times.

Question.—Is it necessary to flog them as often as once a week? As often as once a fortnight?

Answer.—I cannot say.

Question by Chairman.—What is Captain Alexander's conduct among the prisoners under his charge?

Answer.—He is sometimes rough and sometimes pleasant.

Question.—Have you seen him rough without provocation?

Answer.—Well, the Captain has a good deal to excite and provoke him; but I have seen him speak to and treat the prisoners harshly when I thought there was no occasion for it.

Question by Mr. Ward.—Don't you know that the Captain has an excited manner, and when he swears like a sailor, oftentimes he does not mean anything?

Answer.—I don't know.

By Captain Alexander.—Did you ever, Mr. Crow, regret a punishment you saw inflicted on a prisoner at the Castle, and thought it was wrong?

Answer.—I have, sir.

Question.—Have not you, Crow, exulted over the seizure of liquor from poor women at the depots, when you caught them smuggling it into the city?

Answer.—Yes, sir. That was my business, sir.

Question by Chairman.—Did you see the whipping of a man for knocking the eye out of another man?

Answer.—Yes, I was ordered up along with other officers to witness it.

Question.—Was it a powerful man who laid the blows on?

Answer.—Yes, sir; about the strongest man they could get. They gave him I don't know how many lashes.

Question.—Was the thong made of heavy leather?

Answer.—Yes, sir, a heavy thick strap.

Question.—Was the man whipped tried by the court martial, or was he lashed by Captain Alexander's order alone?

Answer.—I think it was by Captain Alexander's order.

By Captain Alexander.—Mr. Crow, do you like Caphart?

Answer.—I do not, sir.

Question.—Haven't you had a quarrel with him?

Answer.—I have, sir.

G. W. BLAND was recalled to the stand.

Question by Chairman.—Do you know Caphart?

Answer.—Only since I have been at the prison.

Question.—What is his general conduct towards the prisoners?

Answer.—Very rough and uncouth.

Question.—Did you ever hear him express regrets at their harsh treatment?

Answer.—No. On the contrary I always found him willing, and assisting to carry out the tyrannical orders of Captain Alexander.

Question.—Did he exult over it, or appear gratified?

Answer.—I can't say as to that, Colonel.

Question.—How long have you known Caphart?

Answer.—Four or five months, I reckon.

Question.—Were you present at the whipping of the two prisoners referred to by the other witnesses?

Answer.—I was, sir.

Question.—Who did the whipping?

Answer.—Two men did the whipping; one laid it on light, and the other very heavy. It was in the case of an old man named Mitchell, who had been badly beaten, or in a case of stealing money from prisoners.

Question.—The prisoners you saw whipped, were they Confederate soldiers?

Answer.—They were, and I don't think they were whipped by order of the court martial.

Question.—Do you know anything of the case of George Wright, a deranged prisoner?

Answer.—Yes. I found him lying down behind a door in the prison room, mired in his own filth, with no clothing on but a short swallow-tailed coat. He was completely covered with scabs and vermin. Some of the prisoners said he had been lying there a week and more. I took him up into the hospital, and treated him medically.

Question.—What is Captain Alexander's treatment of prisoners under his charge?

Answer.—He is in some instances very kind, and in others very different.

Question.—With or without provocation?

Answer.—I can't say, but whether with provocation or not, he might treat prisoners as an officer should treat them.

Question.—Were you ever in the room where the prisoners are confined?

Answer.—Yes, I was in there every day.

Question.—Did the prisoners ever assault, or throw beef bones at you?

Answer.—No, not to my knowledge.

Question.—Did you ever see them throw beef bones at any body?

Answer.—No, I never did.

Question.—How many prisoners do you know to have been killed at the Castle?

Answer.—I can't say, as I was only there five months. One or two killed in that time.

Question by Captain Alexander—Mr. Bland, is there not a place in the Castle called the "sick bay," where the warden puts the prisoners who need to be examined by the surgeon?

Answer.—I know there is such a place.

Question —Is it not the duty of the surgeon to look after these sick cases, and have them removed to the hospital?

Answer.—Yes, it is his duty I believe.

Question.—Have you not made threats of personal violence towards me?

Answer.—I have not, sir.

Question.—Don't you know the cause of Wright's dementedness, or insanity?

Answer.—Yes. Masturbation.

Question.—When you were put in the cell by my order, were you not possessed of a candle and a bottle of whiskey?

Answer.—Yes, sir, I was.

Question by Mr. Ward.—Was the cell not naturally lighted?

Answer.—Yes, through the key hole.

Question.—Do you not harbor an animosity against Captain Alexander?

Answer.—That makes no difference just now. I will tell you: once the Captain sent a negro boy with a bottle to the steward's hospital room, for a bottle of whiskey. My orders were to give nothing of the kind out, and I so informed Captain Alexander. He then wrote me an order for the whiskey, and I wrote in reply that it could not be done. Captain Alexander then sent for me to come to his room. I went to his room, and there was a little dinner party going on. He asked me to sit down, and after I rose, asked me to furnish whiskey for the party, and I told him I could not. He said: "Suppose a man was suffering from a broken leg, and I was to order you to furnish whiskey for his relief, and you refuse, I would put you in the cell." I was afterwards put in the cell for refusing to prescribe for a patient, because I was not a graduated physician, and knew nothing about the disease.

George W. Thomas, sworn.

By Chairman of Committee.—Mr. Thomas, state what you know concerning the treatment of prisoners in Castle Thunder, and any other circumstances bearing on this investigation.

Answer.—I am from Henrico county, and have been a detective to Captain Alexander since the 13th of March, last year. The general treatment of the prisoners I must say is good, as far as my knowledge extends. Two classes of desperados are to be found in the Castle; one from far down South, and the other from Baltimore; the "wharf rats," of New Orleans, and the plugs from Baltimore. A third class is the inoffensive soldiers, who are the great majority.

Question.—Is, in your opinion, the conduct of the officials towards the prisoners humane and kind?

Answer.—Generally kind, except on occasions.

Question.—On what occasion was that?

Answer.—When the prisoners were put in the back yard as a punishment for outrages; a committee among the prisoners, robbing and beating the more inoffensive of them. I looked into the yard, and seeing the prisoners suffering, I reported the condition of the prisoners to Captain Alexander, and he had them brought immediately. Some of the prisoners were warmly clad, but the more desperate of the prisoners generally stole the blankets from the others.

Question.—Where did Captain Alexander receive his orders for the punishment of the prisoners?

Answer.—From General Winder, I think.

Question.—How often were the prisoners put out into that yard?

Answer.—Only on that one occasion that I recollect.

Question.—Had they any blankets?

Answer.—Some of them had, but the strongest, and more desperate got them.

Question.—Was there any covering to the yard to shelter them from the storm?

Answer.—No, sir.

Question.—What is your duty in connection with the prison?

Answer.—I am a detective.

Question.—Are all of the prisoners without blankets?

Answer—No, sir, not all. Men go in there, and their blankets are taken from them by the desperados to make ropes wherewith to escape.

Question.—Are there any benches or seats in the prison room?

Answer.—No sir, nothing of the kind; they would break and burn them up if there was.

Question.—Have you seen men whipped there?

Answer.—I have on one or two occasions.

Question.—Was the punishment inflicted by order of General Winder?

Answer.—It was by his order, which was carried by Caphart. There were eight of them whipped on one occasion. Some two or three were struck a dozen or more blows; others were let off with less.

Question.—What other kind of punishment did you ever see inflicted there? Did you ever see prisoners wearing barrel shirts?

Answer.—Yes, sir, I have.

Question.—Did you ever see men tied up by the thumbs?

Answer.—No, sir, I never did

Question.—Have you known men to be killed there?

Answer.—Yes, several were killed there.

Question.—Do you know the circumstances?

Answer.—General Winder's orders were, after the discovery of the plot to escape, were to fire upon any prisoner thrusting his head from the windows in defiance of the guard, or attempting to escape.

Question.—Do you the think the men shot and shot at, could not have been recaptured without shooting?

Answer.—I know of one instance myself, in the case of Campbell, a deserter, who escaped, and he led me a hard race. I fired at him twice, and he would have escaped, but for the guard coming up in his front.

Question.—Do you know of any cases of whipping at the prison?

Answer.—Yes, several cases. One case, that of an old man, Captain Alexander interested himself very much in because of his age, and through his influence with General Winder, got the sentence of the court martial remitted.

Question by Captain Alexander.—Thomas, do you think I am a cruel man?

Answer.—No, sir, I do not.

Tuesday, April 14th, 1863.

GEORGE W. THOMAS was called:

Question by Chairman of Committee.—Do you know anything of Caphart?

Answer.—I am associated with him as a detective.

Question.—Is he kind and humane?

Answer.—I have seen him treat prisoners with unnecessary harshness and cruelty, I thought.

Question.—Do you think his rough deportment natural with him?

Answer.—He has a rough way and is fond of talking.

Question.—Does he seem to regret the punishment of any prisoner.

·*Answer.*—Caphart has filled the office of jailor to prisons for a great number of years, and in the habit of dealing with bad fellows, he has, perhaps, grown callous and unfeeling.

Question.—Have you ever heard him regret or exult over the punishment of any prisoner?

Answer.—I couldn't say he was a kind man, especially to bad prisoners. Never saw him exult over the punishment of any man, even the hardest villains, with which he has to do. He viewed it in the light of a moral corrective. Towards these he was rather rough. I have heard him curse them, but at such times he had provocation. The prisoners often brick-batted the sentinels; they never threw bones at me; they threw bones at Caphart, because they hated him generally. He is not popular with the prisoners.

Question.—If Caphart had been kind to them do you think they would throw beef bones at him?

Answer.—I can't say as to that. I have seen them throw missiles at the sentinels.

Question.—How are the prisoners clad, generally?

Answer—I have seen some badly clothed, but not more indifferently than at other prisons. Some of the prisoners steal from each other. To relieve their destitution, after the battles around Richmond, Capt. Alexander sent out men to gather up the clothing and blankets from the battle fields to clothe the prisoners, who were destitute.

Question.—Was sufficient clothing obtained in that way to clothe all the destitute prisoners.

Answer.—I can't say that every one was furnished; but a great many were.

Question.—Have you seen a prisoner with more than one suit of clothing.

Answer.—Yes; some of them have not many.

Question.—Do you know such a man as George Wright, once a prisoner in the castle?

Answer.—Yes, sir. He was in the hospital when I saw him. His condition was very bad.

Question.—Do you know anything of a deranged Yankee prisoner who was brought from the Libby prison to the castle, and shot in attempting to escape?

Answer.—Yes. He was brought from the Libby prison for safe keeping, having attempted to get out of that place. He was shot at the castle in attempting to run the sentinel. The sentinels had been changed, and the sentinel who shot him did not know, I think, that he was crazy. I don't know whether Captain Alexander was present there or not

Cap'ain Alexander.—No, Mr. Chairman, I was not at the castle at that time.

Question.—What officer received him?

Answer.—I don't know, sir.

Question.—Was it not the duty of the officer who received him to notify all that he was deranged?

Answer.—I think it should have been done.

Question.—Have you seen barrel shirts worn by the prisoners?

Answer.—Yes; two of them by sentence of the court martial.

Question.—When soldiers are arrested on the street and taken to the castle is it customary for an examination to be made into the charges against them?

Answer.—They are never arrested except without papers, and the returns are made every morning to the Provost Marshal and General Winder.

Question.—Then you put them all in among the wharf rats of New Orleans and the plug uglies of Baltimore?

Answer by Mr. Ward.—If the committee will allow me, I will explain that point. When men are arrested on the street and elsewhere, and sent to the prison, their papers are examined; if regular, they are discharged; if irregular, they are put back until a case can be substantiated or disproved. If the prisoners are sent by the Provost Marshal or General Winder, the commandant of the prison has no authority to discharge, and they are put back. If, at the expiration of a reasonable time, their case remains undisposed of, a letter detailing the facts is forwarded, asking an investigation. Some prisoners have remained in the prison a long time, it is true, the difficulty of getting testimony and collecting witnesses operating against an early investigation. Again, instances have occurred where they have been taken out on writs of *habeas corpus.*

Question.—Are not a great many soldiers taken up and confined there who have merely overstaid their furlough.

Answer by Mr. Ward.—Yes. Men are sent there frequently from the Provost Marshal or General Winder's office, with an order to the effect—"Confine these men and send them to their regiments;" and such men are sent daily to the army, or to Sergeant Crow, at the barracks, or under a guard and escort of the commandant of the prison post.

Question.—You turn the prisoners all in together; the desperadoes with the inoffensive soldiers?

Answer.—There are four or five large rooms for their accommodation, and we discriminate as much as possible in our classification of them.

Question by Capt. Alexander.—Mr. Thomas, have I anything in the world to do with the clothing of prisoners?

Answer.—I think not, unless it was a voluntary act.

Question by Mr. Ward.—Have you been in the army; are not the prisoners in Castle Thunder clothed and fed as well as the soldiers now in the army?

Answer.—I should say fully as well.

Question.—Has not Capt. Alexander exerted himself to clothe the more destitute of them?

Answer.—Yes; I know of many instances of it.

Question by Chairman of Committee.—Do you know Mr. Bland?

Answer.—I don't know much about him.

By Capt. Alexander.—Is Bland a drinking man?

Answer.—I dont know anything about him.

By Mr. Ward—If prisoners were put in Caphart's charge, do you think he would beat them if they would go along quietly and peaceably?

Answer.—I don't think he would.

By Capt. Alexander.—Don't you think there are as hard cases here as anywhere else?

Answer.—Yes, indeed; it would be hard to match.

Stephen B. Childrey, sworn:

Question by Chairman.—What is your position at prison?

Answer.—I am the commissary of the prison.

Question.—What is the general treatment of the prisoners confined there?

Answer.—Good, very good; good as persons in the same situation could be treated.

Question.—Did you ever see any whipping there without the authority of a court martial?

Answer—I never saw any of the prisoners whipped.

Question.—What is the general deportment of the officers towards the prisoners; is it kind?

Answer.—As kind as could be expected. Of course harsh measures have to be used sometimes.

Question.—What is the necessity or excuse for rough language?

Answer.—Because they have some very rough characters to deal with. If they were treated differently they would run over them, and take the prison.

Question.—You have never seen any whipping there?

Answer.—No.

Question.—Seen any other kind of punishment inflicted?

2

Answer.—I have seen prisoners " bucked." They were of the more desperate characters.

Question—Do you know of any prisoners being killed there ?

Answer.—I know of one man dying from the effects of a beating at the hands of some of the prisoners, and I know of another who was shot by the guard in attempting to escape.

Question.—Do you think it was absolutely necessary to shoot this man to have recaptured him ?

Answer—I suppose it was.

Question.—Was the man outside the building when fired upon and killed ?

Answer.—No, sir; he was on the balcony of the second story on Cary street, about jumping down. The sentinel was on the pavement below him.

Question.—Do you know anything about a crazy man who was shot in attempting to escape ?

Answer.—Yes; I heard of the circumstance.

Question.—Do you know anything about the case of George Wright, a prisoner, and his condition when sent to the hospital?

Answer.—Yes, his condition was very bad. I furnished him with clothing, but he would tear the clothes off his person.

Question.—In what condition was he when removed to the hospital?

Answer.—He was travelling about the prison like the other prisoners, but in a demented state of mind. I gave him his food. No filth is allowed to collect in the prison. It is, I will venture to say, one of the cleanest prisons in the State. Captain Alexander is as particular in this respect as any man I ever saw. His usual disposition, when not provoked, is kind and urbane.

Question by Mr. Ward..—You are the Commissary of the prison, are you not ?

Answer.—I am.

Question.—And as such you came in contact with the prisoners a great deal ?

Answer.—Yes, sir.

Question.—From your knowledge, what is the character of the prisoners, or some of them?

Answer —I consider them desperate indeed.

Question.—Did they ever make threats towards you ?

Answer.—Yes; the whipping had an excellent effect on them. They are getting worse now again since the law was passed by Congress abolishing whipping in the army. Something will have to be done to stop their insubordination.

Question.—You know about the clothing collected by Captain Alexander for the use of prisoners ?

Answer.—Yes, I distributed the clothing to the prisoners. I am at liberty to sell them anything in the way of food, luxuries or necessaries; anything they want if they have money to buy. I consider their rations better in quantity and quality than the soldiers in the field.

Question by Chairman of Committee.—Do you know anything about the whipping at the prison ?

Answer.—I never saw any whipping, although it was done.

Question.—Do you know anything about the shooting of prisoners?

Answer.—Yes, sir.

Question—Who gave the order to shoot the prisoners?

Answer by Captain Alexander.—I gave the order to the sentinels, based on the orders of General Winder. I was not at the prison when the shooting occurred, but it is a general standing order to shoot at prisoners cursing or abusing the sentinels from the windows.

Question by Captain Alexander.—Mr. Childrey, do you consider me a cruel man?

Answer.—I do not; but I consider you a positive man—one who wants discipline and orders carried out.

Question.—How many poor women am I not feeding from the milk obtained at the castle?

Answer.—Yes. I know you are supplying a good many.

Question.—Did I not start a hospital and place my wife in it to attend to the sick and wounded?

Answer.—Yes; I knew that Captain.

Question.—And did the Government ever pay me one cent for my money expended?

Answer.—Not that I am aware of.

BALDWIN T. ALLEN, sworn.

Question by Chairman of Committee.—What is your position at Castle Thunder?

Answer.—I am warden.

Question.—What is the treatment of the prisoners?

Answer.—That is rather a comprehensive question. In answering it I must take into consideration the character of some of the prisoners. The commandant has found it necessary to enforce very rigid rules. If they had been less rigid, he would have been unable to keep one of them there.

Question—Does Captain Alexander and the other officers speak kindly or roughly to the prisoners?

Answer.—I don't know of any officer being unkind to well behaved prisoners

Question.—Have you seen whipping there without order of a court martial?

Answer.—I have seen whipping inflicted, but whether with or without the order of court martial, I cannot say.

Question.—Do you know that General Winder gave the order or not.

Answer—I heard so; but I am not positive by whose authority it was done.

Question.—Did you ever see any whipping?

Answer.—Yes; I have seen fifty lashes laid on by order of the court martial.

Question.—Have you seen persons receive six, eight and ten lashes?

Answer.—Yes; frequently.

Question.—Were the men you saw whipped Confederate prisoners, and soldiers of the Confederate service?

Answer.—I think not. I think they were Yankee deserters.

Question.—Were any of them Confederate soldiers?

Answer.—I can't say; but I can get the names to-morrow.

Question.—Do you know anything about the killing of some prisoners?

Answer.—Yes. Last fall, a Yankee deserter, who was deranged, attempted to run the guard and was killed. Another was killed recently in attempting to escape. His name was Charles Carroll, and he was a Confederate soldier.

Question.—Have you ever seen men wear barrel jackets?

Answer.—Yes, sir.

Question—Have you known prisoners to be put out in the prison yard, without fire or shelter in cold weather?

Answer.—Yes. Several months ago. Their offence was robbing and stealing, breaking windows, and gross violation of the rules.

Question.—How long did they remain there?

Answer.—All one day and night, and part of another day.

Question.—Any other instance?

Answer.—The next time the prisoners were put into the back yard, it was in October or November. They had no covering or shelter except their blankets and clothing.

Question.—You say you found out they were suffering. Suppose you had not taken them in promptly, what do think would have been the consequences?

Answer.—I suppose they would have been cold. They could have stood it though. Our soldiers stand it. They had fuel to make a fire.

Question.—Of those placed in the yard last fall, do you know of any who were taken sick afterwards?

Answer.—Some of them may have been sick, but whether from that cause or not I can't say.

Question.—Did you ever see men tied up by the thumbs?

Answer.—Yes; once or twice I saw men tied by the thumbs.

Question.—What was their offence?

Answer.—Stealing, etc.

Question.—Were they Confederate prisoners?

Answer.—Yes.

Question—Who was one?

Answer.—Martin Darby, a young man twenty-five years of age. He was tied up several hours.

Question.—Have you seen men bucked there?

Answer.—Yes, and helped to buck a good many of them myself.

Question.—What was their crime?

Answer.—For various offences. And I may say here that all the punishment inflicted is necessary to keep up the dicipline of the prison.

Question.—Did you ever see the hands of any of the men tied up, black from the stagnation of the blood in them?

Answer.—Yes I have, frequently, I think.

Question.—Did you ever see men hand-cuffed, and their hands bloody from the effects of the tying up?

Answer.—Yes, one was named William Campbell. He slipped **up** his hand-cuffs to his elbows, I believe to cause stagnation of the blood.

Question by Mr. Ward.—You are the warden?

Answer.—Yes, and in that capacity I am generally among the prisoners.

Question.—What is the character of some of the men confined there?

Answer.—I consider many of them the most desperate men in the Southern Confederacy. It would not do to treat them leniently.

Question.—Are not all picked up and put together in these rooms appropriated to the prisoners?

Answer.—But we try to separate the quiet from the quarrelsom prisoners.

Question.—Have you seen prisoners there with one suit on constantly?

Answer.—A change of clothing is beneficial to the health and comfort of the prisoners, but few of them had it.

Question.—Is it a rare or common case for the prisoners to be whipped?

Answer.—Rather rare; but it has had a beneficial effect wherever it has been done.

Question by Captain Alexander.—They say you left. George Wright lay for two weeks in the prison room, sick, without attending to his wants?

Answer.—I think there must be some mistake about that. I go around every morning and call the breakfast roll, and when I find a man down by sickness, I take his name and report him to the surgeon.

Question by Captain Alexander.—I handle a great many prisoners, do I not, but whipping is comparatively rare?

Answer.—Yes, it is for so many.

Question by Mr. Ward.—Are not the prisoners in the Castle constantly changing?

Answer.—Yes; those there to-day are sent off to-morrow.

Dr. LUNDIE, sworn.

Question by Chairman of Committee.—State to the committee what you know of the condition and treatment of prisoners at Castle Thunder?

Answer.—I know nothing particular about the military conduct of the prison. I have been there to get prisoners out, and have received notes from the prisoners. I have been through the prison and hospital, and the condition of the hospital and prison apartments were much better than I expected to find. Below there is a good conduct for carrying off the filth, but the building is not well ventilated, but that is the fault of the building. The hospital is clean beyond comparison, and the surgeon, from what I saw, pays all the necessary attention. While there I saw an enclosure, the back yard, containing a large number of prisoners. They were in a most woeful state, as regards clothing and comfort, and I remarked that it looked like pandemonium. The prisoners were growling and cursing, and I heard the clanking of the chains. One of them accosted me as I passed along, and asked me to get him out. I saw Captain Alexander and asked him to let the fellow out. Captain Alexander remarked, "to keep order here *I have had to kill ten men !*

Captain ALEXANDER here explained that he had used the expression "killed ten men" in a jocose manner, in response to Dr. Lundi's remarks.

Wednesday, April 15, 1863.

The examination of witnesses for the government was resumed.

T. J. KIRBY, sworn.—I am at present an inmate of Castle Thunder, where I have been held a prisoner as a spy for some months past. I am an Englishman, a resident of Niagara, Canada, where I have a wife and children. I came through the lines on business with the government, which will be explained as I proceed. God knows I wish to go back there!

Question by Chairman of Committee.—State what you know about the treatment of the inmates of the prison.

Answer.—At times I have known Captain Alexander to be extremely kind to prisoners; at times the very opposite, extremely harsh and domineering. I have been the recipient of his kindnesses, and on the contrary, I have received treatment from him which to describe (witness excited) I would prefer being interrogated as I proceed.

Chairman of Committee.—Go on and give your testimony in your own way.

Question.—Is Captain Alexander kind?

Answer.—I consider him the very opposite of kindness, and it is so as a general rule. I myself have experienced some of his inhumanity.

Question.—What is the character of his usual intercourse with prisoners?

Answer.—At times he is kind, and at other times extremely rough and uncouth; then kind again, and then rough, as the fit takes him. Simply for going into the hospital by order of the surgeon in charge, Dr Coggin, Captain Alexander threatened to put me in the cell. I was ordered to the hospital by the surgeon to be treated for an effection of the throat. I was requested, or rather invited by Dr. Coggin to visit the hospital daily for medical treatment, also to wile away a few moments of my confinement in pleasant conversation. This privilege was refused me by Captain Alexander, with the threat if I violated his instructions, he would put me in the cell. I am in the hospital now. I was taken from cell No. 3, last Friday, and given the range of the citizen's room. On Monday morning following, while engaged in cleaning my teeth at the pump, the prisoner Campbell being present, Captain Alexander came up to his room. We were talking together of the Captain, and matters about the Castle, and as Captain Alexander came up I turned on my heel to enter my room, saying to Campbell, (suiting the action to the words,) "I have no more respect for Captain Alexander than I have for my *royal Bengal stern.*" I immediately went to my room, and the officers came and took me out, and confined me again in cell No. 3, a room about fifteen feet square, and one window therein, which was covered with boards. I had belonged to a mess in the prison room, and the mess resolved to supply me with my meals. Mr. Allen, the warden, refused to let me have the food sent me, and sent it back. I wrote a note to the mess, and learned that it was refused. I was not allowed to purchase anything from the commissary; I asked for rations and they were refused me. I had nothing to eat from Friday morning to Saturday sometime during the day.

Question.—On what charge are you confined?

Answer.—I have been in prison since the 8th day of November last, on suspicion of being a spy. I applied for, and obtained a writ of *habeas corpus*, and on the 6th of March. Mr. Aylett, the counsel for the Confederate States, closed the case, announcing that no evidence had been adduced to hold me on the charge. On the 11th of March, judgment was rendered in the case by Judge Lyons, and I was informed that I was at liberty to return to the North by flag of truce, which I refused to do, &c., &c.

Question.—What is Captain Alexander's treatment of the other prisoners under his charge?

Answer.—Captain Alexander has his favorites. There are prisoners there whose sentences of court martial, condemning them to wear ball and chain, have not been carried out. I know of two instances, and others have been told me by the prisoners. Any person or prisoner could be Captain Alexander's favorite if he would become his pimp. I could have been one I reckon.

Question.—Relate what instances you know of sentences not being carried out.

Answer.—I know of one young man who was sentenced by court martial to wear a ball and chain, whose sentence was not carried out. He was sentenced to ball and chain and hard labor. He was a fine young man, and I assisted him to write a letter to the President of the Confederate States asking a commutation of the sentence. The charge against him was assaulting his superior officer and desertion. He was in the citizens' room and never had the ball and chain on.

Question.—Did you ever see any Confederate soldiers whipped there?

Answer.—I have seen several whipping operations.

Question.—Without the order of a court martial?

Answer—I don't know. One James McLashen, I was told, was whipped twelve lashes for being quarrelsome in the prisoners' room. I have seen Yankee prisoners whipped for quarreling. I saw four whipped at one time. I was not where I could see at all times. I think two were whipped without the order of the court martial. They were whipped on the bare back, with a leather strap. Do not know that the lash drew blood; heard that it did in one instance,

Question —What other kinds of punishment have you seen inflicted.

Answer.—I have seen prisoners bucked. One in the condemned cell was bucked for speaking to persons in the citizens' room.

Question.—How long do they remain bucked?

Answer.—I have seen them part of two days in that condition.

Question.—Have you seen men wear barrel shirts?

Answer —Yes; I have seen two prisoners with them on about the prison.

Question.—Is the punishment of the shirt severe?

Answer.—No, not painful; not so severe as either thumbing or bucking. The humiliation is greater than the punishment.

Question.—Have you seen any thumbing?

Answer.—Yes, I have seen prisoners tied up by the thumbs as high as they could reach on their tip-toes. They were tied with a small sized whip cord.

Question.—How many hours have you known them to remain in that condition.

Answer.—I have known them to remain in that condition from morning until night.

Question.—Did you ever examine to see if any blood was drawn by the cord?

Answer.—Once I did. The prisoner had pulled and loosened the cord, and his thumbs were black and blue. He didn't complain of pain, but rather took it as a good joke. I have seen men tied up around a post so tightly that they couldn't lie down or sit down. In one instance, I was told that it was the orders of Captain Alexander that they should remain so all night, but some of the officers had let them down so they could sit and lie down.

Question.—What was the crime?

Answer.—Attempting to bribe the guard, I believe.

Question.—Is the foregoing all the instances you know of?

Answer.—They are all I can recall at present.

Question.—How many prisoners were put into the yard on one occasion?

Answer.—All in room No. 2—about one hundred.

Question.—How long did they remain there?

Answer.—For several days, I think. It was in the latter part of November or December. Their offence was putting powder in the stove.

Question.—Were any of them sick afterwards?

Answer.—I cannot say, but I understood some were ill from the effects of the exposure. They had neither covering, fire, nor shelter, except the high walls, and it was raining part of the time.

Question.—Did Captain Alexander give an order to have a fire built in the the yard?

Answer.—I never heard of any.

Question.—How many days were they kept there?

Answer.—Four or five, I understood.

Question.—Were any men shot at the prison?

Answer.—Yes, I have heard of men being shot and shot at for putting their heads out of the window. I, myself, was threatened with shooting. I know Captain Alexander gave an order to the guard to shoot me while I was looking out of an open window once. I drew down the window without moving my head and defied them. I remonstrated with Captain Alexander, and told him my head was not outside of the window, and neither was it.

Question.—Are there any female prisoners?

Answer.—Yes, two, I believe.

Question.—Do you know anything of their treatment?

Answer.—No, only what has been told me.

Question by Mr. Ward.—Mr. Kirby, where are you from?

Answer.—From Niagara, Canada, sir, and have been confined eight months in the citizens' room.

Question.—What were you sent from that room for?

Answer.—A difficulty I had with the Captain, I suppose. We were ordered to scrub and prepare the room for the visit of the inspection committee, and the guard would allow but two of us to go to the pump for water at one time. I remonstrated with Captain Alexander when he called me "a damned son of a bitch," and I called him "a damned coward." I was put in the cell, but that night ordered back to the citizens' room. I apologized for my conduct.

Question.—Then you were put out of the citizens' room last Friday.

Answer.—Yes; my difficulty with Captain Alexander caused it.

Question.—You have a good room and a good bed?

Answer.—Yes. The captain hasn't taken them away yet, but I am not indebted to him for my bed?

Question by Capt. Alexander.—You say I didn't carry out the sentence of Leary, who was condemned to wear ball and chain?

Answer.—No, you did not.

Question.—Did not you yourself petition the President for his reprieve? And did not you sit down in my office and write a letter to the President for Leary concerning his case? And did I not allow you to receive your meals from the hotels and faro banks, and gave you many privileges not enjoyed by the other prisoners?

Answer.—Yes, captain, you did all that.

Question.—You say Mr. Allen's treatment of the prisoners is inhuman?

Answer.—He is generally intoxicated, and it is the merest exception in the world that I ever got a kind answer out of him.

Question by Committee.—What is your opinion of Caphart?

Answer.—I consider him in all respects a vile, low, inhuman person.

Question.—Do you find prisoners like kind and humane officers?

Answer.—I have heard prisoners say they could have escaped at times when it was Mr. Rigg's night on, but they would not do it for fear of compromising his character. All the officers are down on him. I have known the Captain to treat him kindly, and at other times snubb him.

Question.—Do you know Mr. Bland?

Answer.—Yes, his deportment is generally kind.

Question.—Do you know about the case of George Wright?

Answer.— Yes, but I never saw him until I saw him in the hospital.

Question.—Are you, as a prisoner, allowed to see persons from without the prison?

Answer.—Once Hon. Mr. Boteler called to see me, and I was refused an interview with him. I have sent for persons who have been refused to see me. I have been allowed to communicate with counsel several times under seal, and this privilege was also stopped. I once gave a letter to Mr. Riggs to carry to the Captain to read. He said it must go to General Winder, and I gave it to Mr. Ward. On Sunday morning following, some four or five days after, Mr. Ward said he had gin the letter to Captain Alexander.

Question.—What became of the letter?

Answer.—I don't know, sir.

Captain Alexander.—Mr. Chairman shall I send to General Winder's and get it. The letter is on file there?

By Mr. Ward.—There is an order from General Winder that all communications from the prison shall go through his office. Accordingly all letters from the prisoners are put in a box, and taken up to General Winder daily.

Question by Committee.—What did you come here for, Mr. Kirby?

Answer.—I had special business to the Confederate government.

Question.—Was that business made known on your arrival here?

Answer.—It was.

Question.—Are the authorities aware of your arrest?

Answer.—They are.

JOHN SHEHAN, sworn.

Question by Committee.—You are a prisoner at the Castle and a Confederate soldier?

Answer.—Yes, sir.

Question.—What is the treatment of the prisoners generally at the Castle?

Answer.—In a majority of cases I think they are treated kindly. Men are whipped there. I have seen them whipped without the sentence of the Court Martial. Captain Alexander I saw present at the whipping.

Question.—How many lashes were laid on?

Answer.—From six to eight lashes, I should judge. They were laid on hard. The offence in one case was rioting and fighting in the prison room.

Question.—Have you seen any " bucking " there?

Answer.—Yes, and men whipped who were Confederate soldiers. The " bucking " was for the rioting in the prison. I have known men to remain " bucked " as long as four hours.

Question.—Have you seen prisoners tied up by the thumbs?

Answer.—Yes, I think so. He was a Confederate soldier, belonging to Rogers' cavalry. His offence was thieving, I believe.

Question.—What about the prisoners put out into the yards?

Answer.—It was in November, and they were kept there several days. A few had bed covering. Some were in bad health when put out there, and looked miserable enough. Some were sick immediately after their exposure, and I remember of one dying in the hospital.

Question.—Have you seen any men shot there?

Answer.—Yes, one was Carroll, who attempted to escape.

Queston.—Could he not have been captured without shooting?

Answer.—He was in the act of getting out of a window on to the portico, beneath which was the guard. I think he could have been easily taken without killing.

Question.—Was there any investigation into the shooting?

Answer.—I did'nt hear of any. I have known prisoners to be shot at for putting their heads out of the windows. The orders are to shoot them if they will not obey the sentinels. They have been told that often enough. I have put my head out of the window a thousand times and never was shot at.

Question.—Have you got a cell or "sweat house" for the solitary confinement of prisoners?

Answer.—Yes, it is a room about eight feet square. I was confined there once in irons. I could lay down. There are no windows. There is no protection from either the heat or cold.

Question.—What were you put in the cell for?

Answer.—For going out, as coporal of the prison, and getting drunk. I am in prison for being absent from my regiment without leave. My sentence will be out to-day or to-morrow. I have been in prison six months. I was there one month before any charge was preferred.

Question by Captain Alexander.—You are a sailor, are you not, Shehan?

Answer.—Yes, sir.

Question.—Is it not my habit to treat prisoners kindly?

Answer.—No, sir, it is cruel and inhuman.

Question by Chairman of Committee.—What is Captain Alexander's deportment towards prisoners?

Answer—Sometimes he is kind as can be, and at other times he is the very opposite.

Question.—You know Caphart?

Answer—I knew him in Norfolk. He has little to do with the prison. Never saw him arrest a man.

Question by Mr. Ward.—Has my conduct been kind?

Answer.—Yes, you are a gentleman as far as I know.

Question by Captain Alexander.—Have I not a great deal to provoke and make me angry?

Answer.—Yes, I know you have. You have treated me well. I do not find fault with the harshness of the rules, but it is impossible to keep so many men in perfect order.

CHARLOTTE GILMAN, sworn—I have been in Castles Godwin and Thunder going on twelve months all together, the last time about one month.

Question.—What are you in prison for?

Answer.—I am a witness against George W. Elam for counterfeiting.

Question.—What is the general treatment of the prisoners?

Answer.—I have always been well treated. All the ladies there spoke of Captain Alexander in the highest terms. All like him. I know nothing of the treatment of the other prisoners.

Question by Captain Alexander.—Did I not go to General Winder and get an order for your washing?

Answer.—Yes, you did. You have been very kind; and you let me go out very often.

WILLIAM CAMPBELL, sworn.—I have seen no cruelty on the part of Captain Alexander towards the prisoners. I think I am the only one who ever suffered. I was among the number put into the yard. I was also bucked and put in the yard. The charge against me is desertion. I am from Louisiana.

Question.—Have you been tried by court martial?

Answer.—No sir.

Question.—How long have you been in prison?

Answer.—Only one month the last time. I have escaped three or four times.

Thursday, *April* 16, 1863.

The examination of witnesses was resumed.

V. T. CRAWFORD, sworn.—I am located in Richmond, and am a practicing lawyer. I was admitted to the bar some eight months ago. I know nothing of the treatment of the prisoners confined in Castle Thunder, but I do know something of the conduct of its officers who are called upon to visit the prison in a professional way. After I had visited the prison once or twice without interruption, obstacles began to be thrown in my way. First, an order forbidding conversation between myself and clients, without a third person, in the shape of an officer, being present. At another time I was refused admittance beyond the guard, and all the conversation I could hold with my clients had to be carried on through a wire gauze screen. At another time, Mr. Ward informed me I would have to get an official permit from General Winder to see prisoners. I went to General Winder for the pass, and after some delay I was furnished with a general pass, which had to be renewed on the occasion of every visit. General Winder asked me about the prisioners I wished to see, and said there were some men there whom they did not wish to have counsel. I asked him what men? And he replied, "we have our rights and you yours," and something more which I do not recollect. I have continued visiting the prison up to Tuesday last on a pass, to be admitted at the discretion of the commandant. Day before yesterday I wrote out a pass to admit me to an interview with two prisoners, Georga Summers, and Lieutenant George Brown. I carried it to Captain Winder, in a back room at the headquarters, and he signed it. Both of the men sent letters requesting to see me, six days after that. I never got the letter. Enquired and found he had given it to Mr. Allen, who said he had handed it to Mr. Ward to forward to General Winder. Went to General Winder, but found no letter there. Eight or ten days after that the letter reached me.

Question by Chairman of Committee.—Did Captain Alexander obstruct your intercourse with the prisoners?

Answer.—He told me to do my speaking to them through the guard.

Question.—Did he know your visits were professional ones?

Answer.—Yes, he was well aware of that fact.

Question.—Were not some of your clients citizens?

Answer.—Yes, one. A man named Weeks; was a citizen of Loudoun or Fauquier. He was finally tried and discharged, after an imprisonment of four or five months.

Question.—Do you know anything else bearing on the subject before the committee?

Answer.—I know another affair which first raised my suspicions. I was called professionally to see a soldier named Miller, belonging to Captain Thornton's company of Caroline County. I agreed to undertake his case for fifty dollars, and he said he would give that. Miller was discharged, and when I saw him he said Mr. Ward had told him not to pay me the fifty dollars fee, as he, (Mr. Ward) had done more for him than I had. Previous to this, Miller told Ward to keep a note for sixty-five dollars, and give it to me. I enquired for the note of Mr. Ward, and it was not to be found.

Question.—Did Miller pay Mr. Ward?

Answer.—I cannot say that he did.

Mr. Ward to the Committee.—I deny the statement Mr. Crawford has made. He called on me on one occasion and desired that I should solicit practice for him, or, in other words, take advantage of my position to drum up clients for him at the Castle. He said he understood such a procedure was customary at the Richmond bar, and offered to give me half of the proceeds of such a joint operation. I told him I would not be a party to any such arrangement, that it was unprofessional, and that a party who stooped to it would most certainly loose standing and position at the bar. I did say that in case Mr. Crawford was enquired for I would notify him of it.

Dennis Conners sworn.—I was an inmate of Castle Thunder. I am paroled to report there until I make a choice of the branch of the service I shall enter. I prefer the navy.

Question by Committee.—How were you treated while there?

Answer.—I was taken up on the street late at night by the guard and sent to Castle Thunder as a supposed deserter. I had been drinking. I was put in a dungeon, a small room called the "sweat house." I was kept there from Thursday to Saturday at 3 o'clock, when I was taken up stairs to be flogged, by order of Captain Alexander. I was ordered to take off my clothes, and I stripped. I was tied up by my wrists to a post, and one of the members of Captain

Bossieux's company laid on the lashes, and he would spring on his toes at every lick. Capt. Alexander was present, and told the man with the lash to lay it on to me. That was the only time I was ever whipped.

Question.—Who arrested you?

Answer.—Caphart arrested me. I don't know anything about his general disposition, as he never came among the prisoners much. He looked as if he would treat them rough if he had anything against them. The prisoners all liked Riggs. He could go among them without molestation at all times. Mr. Allen, the warden, is a rough man. I was put into the yard along with the other prisoners. It was for exploding powder in the room. There was no danger of blowing up the building. It was done to frighten some North Carolina soldiers who were lying by the wall asleep.

Question.—Did Captain Alexander find out the guilty parties?

Answer.—No, sir. They were all put down into the yard because none would tell. The orders were to take no blankets or extra covering, but some were lowered from the windows afterwards. Some of the prisoners were in bad health; several died from it, and several were taken into the hospital.

Question.—Had the prisoners any fire in the yard?

Answer.—The commissary gave them some wood, a dozen sticks or so at night, but none in the day time. I don't remember the month but it was in November, I think. It snowed the first night, and the next night it rained. The ground was not very muddy until our feet cut it up.

Question.—Did you see any other whipping there?

Answer.—Oh, yes. I don't know whether by order of court martial or not. I saw ten whipped for being concerned in stealing one coat. All except one were whipped, and he was a Federal prisoner. The others were Confederate soldiers and two Yankee deserters.

Question.—They were whipped because the coat could not be found?

Answer.—They did not know anything about it, I reckon. The coat was found. The prisoner who lost the coat selected the prisoners whom he suspected to be whipped. Captain Alexander was present, and ordered the lashes to be laid on hard.

Question—How many lashes did they strike each?

Answer.—Well, some six, some eight, and some twelve.

Question.—Have you seen any men "bucked" there?

Answer.—Yes, for such offences as disobeying orders, cutting the walls, transgressing the rules, &c.

Question.—Is "bucking" severe?

Answer.—No, not very severe.

Question.—Do you know of any men being killed there?

Answer.—Yes, several men were shot.

Question.—Do prisoners who are confined in the "sweat room" suffer much?

Answer.—There is air but no light, and the fare is bread and water. I did not suffer for water. The corporal of the guard brought me water, and I had a bucket for slops. I could go out once a day myself.

Question.—When arrested were you taken before the Provost Marshal or to the Castle?

Answer.—I was taken to the Castle.

By Captain Alexander.—I had your brother Thomas there once, Connor, what was my treatment of him?

Answ r.—Well, Captain, you treated me rather rough.

Question.—Are not all the prisoners glad to see me when I come among them?

Answer.—Yes, because they wanted you to transact some business for them. Sometimes I wanted to get little things in, such as clothing, &c., and I could not get them; and persons wishing to see me have been denied, I supposed, by your order.

MARION C. RIGGS sworn:

Question by the Chairman of the Committee.—What is your position at the Castle, Mr. Riggs?

Answer.—I was warden.

Question.—What is the deportment of Captain Alexander towards the prisoners confined there?

Answer.—I have seen many instances of cruelty by order of Captain Alexander. I regard the treatment of the prisoners by Captain A. and his officers as cruel and inhuman.

Que tion.—Have you seen men whipped there?

Answer.—Yes, on several occasions, some I knew were not by the order of a court martial. They were charged with stealing from other prisoners up stairs. Others were whipped for beating, breaking out of cells, and interfering with the guard, &c.

Question.—What number of lashes did they receive.

Answer.—I have known as many as twelve to be laid on.

Question.—Did you see any bucking done there?

Answer.—Yes, and prisoners put into the back yard and kept there two or three days and nights in succession. It was in cold weather. Some were well provided with clothing. There was no sheltering except the wall, and no extra covering. They were fed on bread and water during that time.

Question.—Do you know of any men dying there after being taken out?

Answer.—I know of none, though several were sick.

Question.—The " sweat house"—do you know of men being confined there?

Answer.—Generally men caught in attempting to escape were put in there on bread and water.

Question.—What is " bucking?" Describe it.

Answer.—It is a severe and degrading punishment. It is done by passing a split across the elbows and tying them beneath the thighs, after the manner of a calf going to market. .

Question.—Were any men shot there?

Answer.—I recollect one man who was shot while rushing past the sentinel out of a cell. He was shot in the enclosed yard. He could have been secured without shooting. He was making his way up stairs, and was fired upon at the foot of the stairs. He died in three or four days. He seemed to be insane.

Question.—What was Captain Alexander's deportment then? Did he seem to regret it?

Answer.—I cannot say.

Question.—What was the man's name; was he a Confederate soldier?

Answer.—I never could find out his name. It was in October or November, 1862.

Question.—Was there an investigation into the shooting?

Answer.—I do not know.

Question.—Did Captain Alexander give orders to shoot men attempting to escape?

Answer.—I never heard of such an order.

Question.—Did you hear any regrets expressed among the officers for the shooting of this man?

Answer.—Yes, several, but not Caphart or Allen. I heard the surgeon of the post wasn't in, and sent for Dr. Rucker, a prisoner. I picked him up. He was crazy and no mistake.

Question.—Was it known that he was deranged?

Answer.—I could tell he was. He was brought from the Libby prison where he was fired upon for the same offence, and was killed at the Castle the day he entered.

Question.—What is the general character of Caphart? Is he kind?

Answer.—I would say not; rather brutal. I have known instances when he has been ordered to tie up and buck prisoners, and he seemed to take a special pleasure in it. He would tie them up as tight as possible, and I myself have let them down. I never heard him curse prisoners, but have seen him shake his stick over them when brought in. I never heard him express any regrets for them.

Question.—What of Allen? Is he kind and humane?

Answer.—I never saw him use physical force. I have heard him curse the prisoners.

Question.—Is there any difficulty in managing prisoners?

Answer.—Sometimes there is insubordination. They never resisted me, nor threw beef bones at me, and I was frequently among them.

Question.—Do you think they would be insubordinate if kindly treated?

Answer.—I don't believe they would.

Question.—Are you connected with the prison now?

Answer.—I was discharged on the first of the month, it was said, by the board of Investigating Committee, to reduce force and expenses.

Question.—Do you know at whose instance you were discharged?

Answer.—I do not.

Question.—Are persons allowed to see prisoners?

Answer.—Yes, if they have passes.

Question.—Do you know of obstacles being thrown in the way of attorneys wishing to see clients?

Answer.—I have known instances. They are permitted to go in and stand at a screen window and talk through it.

Question.—Do you consider Allen cruel?

Answer.—Sometimes he is kind, and at other times crabbed. I like him very much.

Question.—Do you regard Captain Alexander as cruel?

Answer.—I have thought his punishments more severe than the cases demanded. He always had some friend whom he shielded.

Question.—Do you know of any cases where the Captain has taken the responsibility of remitting the sentences of court martial?

Answer.—No, sir, I do not. I was connected with the prison six months, and saw punishments once or twice a week.

Question.—Hear of any complaints about food?

Answer.—Yes, there were some complaints. There were plenty of food though; a pound of meat and a loaf of bread each. The floors were swept once or twice a day, and washed once a week, generally on a Saturday.

Question by Captain Alexander.—What are the characters of the prisoners confined there?

Answer.—Very desperate fellows, many of them. I saw the cases of Mitchell and Tyree, who were beaten by them, and the men who were struck by a slung shot. The guilty were afterwards whipped by order from headquarters (Gen. Winder's.) My position was on the same floor with the mass of prisoners.

Question by Captain Alexander—What is the cry when a new prisoner enters?

Answer.—"Fresh fish!" They are then generally beat and robbed if they have anything worth while.

Question by Mr. Ward.—Has Captain Alexander been kind to you and the other officers?

Answer.—Yes.

Question by Captain Alexander.—Do you think I am unkind?

Answer.—Yes, in some instances.

Question by Committee.—When Captain Alexander sent the prisoners into the yard, was it done by order of Gen. Winder?

Answer.—I don't know that it was.

Question.—Was it in the newspapers?

Answer.—Yes, I think it was.

Question.—Do you think Captain Alexander, by nature, a cruel man?

Answer.—Yes. I consider his treatment cruel.

Question.—What do the prisoners think of Captain Alexander?

Answer.—I have heard him spoken of with disrespect.

Captain CYRUS BOSSIEUX sworn.

Question by Committee.—You are stationed at the prison, are you?

Answer.—Yes, sir.

Question.—What punishments have been inflicted there in violation of law?

Answer.—I don't know that I have seen any in violation of law. I know of whippings and buckings, and men being put into the yard to find out the perpetrators of outrages on prisoners.

3

Question.—Have you seen any tied up by the thumbs ?

Answer.—But I have seen them bucked. It is not severe, but is esteemed humiliating. I have seen men tied up to a post; I can't swear that I saw them tied by the thumbs; but the punishment can either be made light or severe. I know one who was tied up for attempting to bribe my guard. The guard told me of it, and I reported the case to Captain Alexander. Captain Alexander ordered him to be handcuffed, and tied to a post. He sent for me and I examined his ropes.. I loosened them, and he was afterwards set at liberty. There were two connected in the bribing, and they were Confederate soldiers.

Question.—Do you know Riggs ?

Answer.—Yes. I do.

Question.—Do the prisoners like him ?

Answer.—Yes, they do, as one of the wardens.

Question.—Do you know Caphart ?

Answer.—I don't think him inhuman, if prisoners don't resist him hard; I don't consider him kind by any means. On one occasion, Caphart, while having two prisoners, Dennis and O'Connor, in charge, one of the prisoners knocked a guard down, and Caphart ordered the guard to fire, which they did not do.

Question.—Do you know of any men shot there ?

Answer.—One of my guard shot a man who was attempting to escape. The orders are not to shoot a man of whom there was a possibility of capturing.

Question.—Were these orders from the Captain ?

Answer—Yes; but I don't know that the orders were peremptory to shoot every one.

Question.—Is there any necessity for shooting deranged men ?

Answer.—I did not see the shooting ; never heard of that ; I did'nt speak of that.

Question.—Did you ever hear of orders to the guard, by the military commandant of prisoners, to kill them were they to put their heads out of the windows ?

Answer.—Persistent effort in that way would ensure their firing upon because it was against the rules.

Question by Captain Alexander.—The night that Riggs and Dillard had the fight, Riggs says I was drunk; was he not drunk or under the influence of liquor?

Answer.—I heard he was, sir.

Question by Captain Alexander.—Do you think I am a cruel man ?

Answer.—No, sir, I do not think so.

Question, continued.—I have sometimes hard cases to deal with ?

Answer.—You have some of the hardest cases in the Confederacy. I have heard of no persons being privately punished; all openly, and exhibitions for the public.

Question.—Has the Captain no disposition to be cruel ?

Answer.—No, sir.

Question.—Nor Caphart ?

Answer.—Good officer, sir.

Question.—Ever see Allen drunk !

Answer.—I have seen him in liquor.

Question.—How many times have you seen Riggs drunk ?

Answer.—He was very drunk once from the way he acted.

Question.—Did he get the mania potu.

Answer.—I don't know.

HENRY EDENBOROUGH, sworn

Question.—What are you?

Answer.—I was a captain in the East India royal navy. I came through from Washington in November last. The Yankees had taken my papers, and I was taken and locked up in Castle Thunder by order of the Secretary of War. I experienced there excellent treatment by Captain Alexander. I had a good room and opportunity to see the treatment of other prisoners; never heard of harsh treatment; never experienced any myself; any person who conforms to the rule will never be harshly treated. I have visited and commanded military prisons in Europe, in Naples, Sardinia, in 1860 and '61 ; have visited and seen the hulks in India and China, and have seen nothing so lenient as at Castle Thunder in America. In regard to the rations, I consider them fine. I got my meals sent frequently from the hotels, and dined there often ; and always got more than I wanted. Nothing was refused to come in to any of the prisoners. Many small favors the prisoners were the recipients of. Men being sent off to their regiments were allowed to go into town, under guard, to get clothing. I have seen prisoners leave the prison who would take an affectionate and cordial leave of the Captain, and express regrets to him at parting.

Question.—Do you know of any soldiers put in as comfortable quarters as you occupied ?

Answer.—Yes; the citizens' room was very comfortable indeed, and I have seen men put there.

Question.—Then it depends on general appearance and conduct how treated ?

Answer.—Yes, it depends upon behavior in a great measure.

Question.—Did the Secretary of War order your release ?

Answer.—No ; my arrest was by order of the Secretary of War, and my release was effected through the courts.

Question by Captain Alexander.—Do you think me a cruel man ?

Answer.—No, not exactly ; but you make men toe the mark.

Question.—Did you ever see Riggs drunk ?

Answer.—Yes, he came in my room once very drunk.

Question by Captain Alexander.—Have you been offered a position in the Confederate army ?

Answer.—Yes, major of artillery.

Question by Committee.—Then you consider the punishments at the Castle humane in the highest degree !

Answer.—Yes, I do, considering.

Question by Committee.—Would you take it as a mild punishment to be stripped naked and whipped upon the bare back without the order of a court martial ?

Answer.—Well, in the service I belonged to, whipping was an ordinary punishment. It was not considered a great indignity in the English service to be whipped with a cat-o-nine-tail.

Question.—Is that all you know?

Answer.—That's all I know.

Wednesday, April 22, 1863.

JOHN ADAMS, sworn.—I am from this city, and have been in Castle Thunder seven months for leaving my regiment without leave, and going home.

Question.—What was your treatment there?

Answer.—Well, I was treated pretty tolerable rough. The charge against me was never established. There was an attempt to bribe the sentinel, and I was taken and handcuffed, and ironed around a post, and tied up by my thumbs with a rope, my toes just touching the floor. I was in that condition for one hour or more, when Captain Bossieux came along and released me. Then I was put into the sweat house, the floor of which was covered with mud and water. I was kept there two days and nights. It was in March, 1862, I think, and very cold. There was no dry spot in it. I could only stand up in it half bent.

Question.—How were you fed?

Answer.—I was'nt fed at all. I got nothing except what I bought from the commissary. I happened to have some money. I was put into the back yard, and kept there a day and a half. I was bucked once, with a relief of fifteen or twenty minutes at intervals.

Question.—Were your wrists tied tight then?

Answer.—Yes, I can show the scars of hand-cuffs on my wrists, now.

Question.—Were you ever before a court martial?

Answer.—Yes. I was sent to wear a ball and chain for six months, and to be sent to my company. The reason I don't go to my company is, the Captain wants me to stay here.

Question.—Are your thumbs swollen from the tying up?

Answer.—Yes; it was very painful. I have seen others tied up like me.

Question.—Have you seen parties whipped without the authority of court martial?

Answer.—Yes; some five or six. Their offence was stealing from other prisoners.

Question.—How many lashes did they receive?

Answer.—Some five or six, and some more. Captain Alexander was present, and said once "dam him, give him hell: If he don't need it now, he will." He seemed to take delight in punishing us; and he had a very rough manner in the administration of his punishments.

Question.—Has his general deportment been such that you consider him cruel and inhuman?

Answer.—Yes, I do; and I think it gave him pleasure to punish the prisoners.

Question.—Do you know anything about the shooting of men at the castle?

Answer.—Yes; I know of the man who was shot at for sitting in the window. The sentinel ordered him to get out of the window. I don't know whether he got out or not, but he fired, and put a buckshot through his hat.

Question.—Was that by order of Captain Alexander?

Answer.—I have heard him tell the sentinel to shoot the first man who put his head out of the window.

Question.—Do you know Caphart?

Answer.—Yes, sir; and he is no gentleman. He is a harsh and cruel man. Mr. Allen is rough-spoken, and I have heard him speak so when a kind word would have done as well.

Question.—Did you ever see Mr. Allen drunk?

Answer.—I have seen him out of the way four or five times. Never saw him so far gone that he could'nt attend to his business.

Question.—Do you know Riggs?

Answer.—Yes; he is a kind man, and all the prisoners like him.

Question.—Do you know prisoners who like Captain Alexander.

Answer.—Yes; some speak in favor of him.

Question.—Do you think if Riggs had commanded there; you would hear of any fighting or throwing of bones?

Answer.—I don't believe they would; we would get along well. I never heard of prisoners who had made their arrangements to escape and would not because it was Riggs' night on.

By Mr. Ward. When you were tied up by the thumbs did you not ask me to let you down?

Answer.—Yes, you let me go.

Question.—Was'nt the rope around your wrists and thumbs, and over the nail, and not around your thumbs?

Answer.—I don't recollect now.

Question.—What about your attempt to bribe the guard?

Answer.—The money was sent to me for that purpose. I had not been accused of stealing.

Friday, April 24th, 1863.

The testimony for the defence was commenced.

Mr. Farhon, M. D., made a statement of facts that fell under his notice while visiting the castle in the capacity of one of the medical committee appointed to inspect the sanitary condition of the prisons and hospitals. The impression made upon his mind was that every care was taken of the prisoners that it was possible to take. This feature, and the well ordered condition of everything about the prison was remarked by all the committee.

Captain JACKSON WARNER, A. Q. M. and A. C. M., sworn.

Question.—How long have you known Captain Alexander?

Answer.—Since June, 1861. Never before.

Question.—Did you ever see him intoxicated?

Answer.—I never saw him drunk; but I suppose he drinks sometimes. I always found him attentive to his duties. I see him twice a
week, or oftener. I never saw or heard of him being drunk.

Question.—What do you think of his treatment of prisoners?

Answer.—I know nothing of his associations with the prison. I
never heard him curse in my life; think he is a member of Church.

Question.—Did you ever see him treat a prisoner roughly?

Answer.—Never in my life.

Question —What are your ideas of the management of the prison?

Answer.—I always thought the prison was managed well, and I
have had opportunities to see and know. I have no prison experience
myself.

Question.—How long have you known Captain Alexander?

Answer.—Since June, 1861; and since that time, intimately so.

Question.—Do you know any instances where Captain Alexander
showed kindnesses to prisoners?

Answer.—Yes, I do. In the case of Mr. Larmadoux, my clerk.
He was put into the castle for drunkenness. He had a sick wife at
home, and I went to Captain Alexander, and, stating the case, asked
him to let him go home, and I would be responsible for his return.
He did so, and the next morning he reported. He was again arrested
when sent to his regiment, and again released on his parole by Capt.
Alexander, upon a statement of facts I represented to him.

Question.—In what rooom was he confined?

Answer.—In the room in which the clerks slept, so he told me.

Question.—Do you know anything in regard to the case of Government property?

Answer.—I never saw any waste. If waste had existed, I would
have taken notice of it, as it is my business.

WILLIAM F. WATSON, Confederate States Commissioner, sworn:

Captain Alexander.—Judge, some complaints have been made of my
treatment of lawyers coming to the Castle on business. You have
been there frequently; tell the committee how you were treated, and
how I deal with the profession.

Answer.—I am a practising lawyer, and have frequently called at
the Castle on business. I have always been treated by Captain Alexander with uniform kindness; not only by the Captain himself but by
all his officers. I had no difficulty at all in gaining access to the prisoner I wished to see. All I had to do, was to go the proper officer
and they were either sent down to me, or I up to them. So far as the
character of the majority of the prisoners are concerned, I must say,
to express it in common parlance, they are a hard crowd. It must require great coolness and determination to manage them. I s Commissioner have had some of them before me.

Question —Do you regard the Captain as a cruel man?

Answer.—No, I should say he was rather of a kindly disposition, rather impulsive. He can manage by an appeal about as well as any official I know.

Question.—Do you think Capt. Alexander a man not to be swayed from his purpose?

Answer.—I consider him impulsive but positive; one to do a thing under the excitement of a moment.

Question.—Do you think the prisoners could be managed better under a milder or kinder man?

Answer.—Mild men are not always the best for such posts, a little blending of the severe is better.

JOHN DEBUTTS, M. D., sworn.

I am Surgeon of Castle Thunder Hospital.—So far as I have opportunities of observation, I regard the management of the prison as good, very good. I have never had any prison experience before.

By Captain Alexander.—Have I not told you, Doctor, that your orders in regard to the sick were supreme?

Answer.—Yes, you have told me so.

Question.—Do you think I am a cruel man?

Answer.—I never saw any cruelty practised by you.

Question.—Doctor, what was Mr. Bland discharged from the post of steward of the hospital for?

Answer.—Moral incompetency, I call it.

Question by Committee. What is moral incompetency?

Answer.—He was in the habit of appropriating the hospital liquor to his own private use. No one else had access to it, for he had the key. I don't know how much was taken, but a great deal more was used than went to the patients.

By Captain Alexander.—Is Kirby, the prisoner, comfortably fixed now?

Answer.—Yes, he has the best room in the prison; the best ventilated and situated.

Question by Chairman.—Has Kirby the privilege of buying his meals?

Captain Alexander to Committee.—Gentlemen, I wish to prove by Dr. De Butts that I never refused an appeal of sickness. When a man is to be branded, I direct the surgeon to indicate where the iron is to be placed, and when men are sentenced to be whipped the lashes are remitted if in the opinion of the surgeon the party's health is unequal to the punishment.

Question by Chairman.—Do you know of any prisoners being placed in the yard of the Castle?

Answer.—Yes, a number were confined there. They were brought in at night. I knew nothing of the whipping; never saw it done. I know of one man who escaped and was shot, and another was shot at for blackguarding the sentinel. His face was lacerated by splinters, and I dressed it for him.

Colonel ROBERT MAYO, member of the Legislature from Henrico county, sworn.

Captain Alexander.—You have known me a long time, Colonel; tell the committee what you know of me.

Answer.—My first acquaintance with Captain Alexander was on an occasion of a visit to him in his official capacity, in relation to some abuse near my residence which he speedily caused to be corrected. I found him pleasant and kind. This was when he was at Castle Godwin. When he moved down to Castle Thunder I saw him oftener. A great many of my neighbors were in the guard, and I was frequently called to see prisoners. I often remarked that I never saw so many prisoners together under the same circumstances kept so ordely. They were as sprightly as any people I ever saw. It was wonderful to me.

Mr. Ward.—Colonel, tell about the shooting you saw there.

Answer.—One day I was about going into the Castle a sentinel was about shooting a prisoner at a window, for a violation of the rules, when Captain Alexander interfered, ordered him to desist, not to shoot, that he would order the prisoner to be put in irons instead. I saw two prisoners shot at the Libby prison, but Captain Alexander had nothing to do with that.

Question by the Committee.—What other kinds of punishment did you see there?

Answer.—I saw prisoners wearing a barrel shirt, but that inflicts no pain.

Question.—Is it not degrading to the soldier?

Answer.—The one I saw did not think so; he was jesting about it.

By Mr. Ward.—From your knowledge of Captain A. and his treatment of prisoners, do you think him a cruel man?

Answer.—I do not consider him a cruel man; by no means. If the prisoners conduct themselves well there is no trouble whatever.

Question.—Do you know Mr. Childrey?

Answer.—Yes, and a more honest and correct man cannot be found in the city of Richmond. I also know Mr. Caphart, and Mr. Thomas, another officer at the prison, and one of my neighbors. I have seen them all in the discharge of their duties, and found them very attentive. I have called on Captain Alexander to send a squad of men to my neighborhood, when disturbed, and peace has been restored.

Captain Thomas P. Turner, commandant of the Libby prison, sworn:

By Captain Alexander.—Captain, describe in your own terms your ideas of my treatment of prisoners.

Answer.—Well, I regard the prison as exceedingly well regulated. The discipline maintained has been good, while the character of the inmates are the worst in the land. I regard none of the means employed to control them too severe or unnecessary punishment.

Question.—What kind of punishment do you inflict when any is necessary?

Answer.—For slight offences I make them " mark time," and for graver offences, I "buck" them.

Question.—Your prisoners are Yankees, and not Confederate soldiers?

Answer.—Yes, sir, all of them.

By Mr. Ward. You have sent your worst cases to the Castle, have you not?

Answer.—Yes, I have.

Question.—Is the order to shoot an escaping prisoner a standing order?

Answer.—No, I make my own orders, and have them approved by General Winder. I would allow no man to be shot who could be caught without shooting. .

Question.—If a prisoner was to attempt to escape from your prison by running up stairs, as one did at the Castle, would you consider it the duty of that sentinel to shoot him?

Answer.—Not unless that man was about to escape, and there was no possibility of capturing him.

Question.—Well, does a prisoner ever escape by running up stairs?

Answer.—Not in my prison, sir.

Question.—Would you investigate a case of the kind?

Answer.—Yes, certainly, and report the facts to headquarters.

Question.—Did you send a deranged man to Castle Thunder, and who was killed there in attempting to escape?

Answer.—No sir, it was done by my predecessor.

Question.—If a deranged man was brought to your prison, would you not consider it your duty to warn all hands that he was deranged, in order to guard against accidents, or to confine him?

Answer.—It would be very difficult to know what to do with him. The deranged man Silas Richmond, who was killed at the Castle, was a Yankee. He passed the guard several times in my prison, but the guard understood he was crazy. As for keeping the prisoners in the yard at the Castle over night, I don't know anything about that.

Saturday, April 25, 1863.

The testimony was resumed for the defence.

Captain Thomas P. Turner, recalled.

Question by Mr. Ward.—Were you ever present at Castle Thunder when punishment was being inflicted?

Answer.—Yes, I witnessed one whipping not by order of court martial. I think General Winder authorized it. Three were whipped, I think for mal-treatment of other prisoners, stealing, &c. The lashes were laid on tolerably hard, one receiving twelve, and the other six and a third only three lashes. The lashes were laid on with a leather strap, about eighteen inches long, and weighing about one pound and a half. The lashes were laid on tolerably hard, but left no mark; the skin was not broken. Captain Alexander had been instructed to administer twelve lashes, but he used his own discretion and lessened the number. After it was over he congratulated the prisoners in the manliness they exhibited, and said he was sorry the necessity for the infliction of such punishment existed.

Question.—Did you hear Captain Alexander say "lay it on harder."

Answer.—No sir. They were tied up by the wrists around a post, except one who said he could not stand it, and he was allowed to clasp his arms around the post. The above was the only punishment I saw inflicted there. I know Captain Alexander well, am often with him, and regard him as a kind man.

Question.—Is Captain Alexander intemperate?

Answer.—I never saw him intoxicated in my life. I have seen him drink. He is a sociable man, and will take a drink with his friends.

Question.—What is the character of the inmates of the Castle; are they mutinous?

Answer.—Their characters are various; some of the most desperate men in the Confederacy are there. I was for a time the officer of that post, and all passed through my hands. Once I ordered the arrest of two of my guard, and sent them to the Castle. They were no sooner put in the prisoners' room than they were set upon, beat, their clothing torn off, and robbed of everything. The offenders in this offence were whipped. I don't think there is a cleaner prison anywhere. It is kept remarkably neat and orderly.

Question.—Did you ever hear any complaints respecting Captain Alexander's conduct?

Answer.—No, sir, not until this committee met. I know he is a strict disciplinarian, and keeps things straight around him. His punishment is not more stringent than necessary, I suppose. At my prison, where all are Yankees, I have no need for such modes of punishment. No robberies are committed among the prisoners, for their money is all taken away from them when they enter, and given back to them when they leave. This is to prevent bribery.

By Mr. Ward.—This plan was for some time in practice at the Castle, but the prisoners would hide it about their persons, and in their boots.

Question.—Have you any instances of bribery?

Answer.—No, nothing positive, though there have been attempts.

Lieutenant DENNIS CALLAHAN, sworn.—I am the adjutant of the Castle, and have been there three months.

Question.—What is the general treatment of the prisoners?

Answer.—In my opinion, judging from the time I have been there, the prisoners are treated as well as they could be under the circumstances.

Question.—What is the character of the prisoners?

Answer.—Some of them are of very bad repute. I have seen whipping and bucking as punishment for stealing.

Question.—Are not the prisoners fed on soldiers rations?

Answer.—Yes, and as far as I know they get more to eat than our soldiers.

Question.—Are not the soldiers among the prisoners as well dressed as the soldiers in the field.

Answer.—As a general thing, I should say they were. The Captain has interested himself in obtaining clothing from the government authorities.

JAMES JENNINGS, sworn.---I have been six months in the Castle, and am from Maryland. I left my company on sick leave, and was walk-ing around getting well when arrested. I broke out after two months confinement, and started for my company, and was arrested and sent back, my company being disbanded.

Question.—Have you been kindly treated?

Answer.—Yes, as well as could be expected.

Question.—Have you been punished?

Answer.—No, sir. I was put in the cell four days, I thought that perfectly right. It was for writing a letter and sending it out of the prison without submitting it to the Captain. The cell is not a comfort-able place; it is dry but cold. I suffered from the cold, and was fed on bread and water. I think I was kept there five days. I thought the letter would go quicker and surer by sending through private hands. I am seventeen years old. I don't know what I am detained for.

JOHN DOYLE, sworn.—I have been in the Castle now four weeks. I don't know Captain Alexander, would not know him if I was to see him. I am treated as well as the others, I reckon. I never was pun-ished; in fact I don't deserve it. I was shot at once in the window, or at least I thought I was shot at; but I don't believe he intended to hit me, for I don't deserve it.

Question.—Didn't a shot go through your hat?

Answer.—Can't tell; there is a hole through it.

JAMES McCLASHER, sworn.—I am a seaman, and came from Wil-mington, N. C. I came here when the war broke out. I have not been treated by Captain Alexander as a man should be treated. I have been tied up and flogged like a negro.

Question.—How many lashes did you receive?

Answer.—Twelve, I think; and by Captain Alexander's order they were laid on as hard as I could well have stood it.

Question.—Was the blood cut out of you?

Answer.—No; but I was black and blue, and was sore for a month afterwards. I was whipped with a strap three inches wide, and the blows were laid on by Caphart. I have been bucked for four hours in front of the office entrance, where everybody could see me. Buck-ing is not painful, but it mortifies and makes one ashamed.

Question —Do you know of any other punishments?

Answer.—Yes; I was shot at once for standing at a window and looking out. The ball passed my head and went up through the hospital, which was full of patients.

Mr. WYNNE, door keeper of the House of Representatives, detailed before the committee some circumstances of his treatment at the prison, when he went down to summon some officers, and the purport of his conversation with several witnesses, which not being to the point here, is omitted.

Monday, April 27, 1863.

Hon. Judge OULD, sworn.

Question by Capt. Alexander.—You, as Judge Advocate of the court martial, can give the committee some idea of the character of the prisoners?

Answer.—The most of the cases brought before me, were cases of desertion, coupled with theft, and cases of insubordination.

Question.—Do you think I am a cruel man?

Answer.—I do not know about that. I do not think you are.

Question.—What do you think about me carrying out an order?

Answer.—Being a military man, you would see any reasonable order carried out. I have conversed at times with persons who have been in Castle Thunder, and have questioned them as to their treatment there. Never heard them mention any cases of cruelty, but generally the reverse. There has been half a dozen sentenced to be shot, and two condemned to be hung. We have never resorted to the death penalty unless the case presented the two aggravated phases, first, desertion, and secondly, desertion in face of the enemy. I know nothing of the punishments by the commandant of the Castle; never visited it in my life, that I know of. In all sentences of court martial the lashes were well laid on, except in one instance.

Lieutenant PETER CALLAHAN, sworn.—Your conduct towards the prisoners has been as kind as it well could be under the circumstances.

Question—What is my conduct towards visitors?

Answer.—I always thought your conduct gentlemanly.

Question.—One of the witnesses swore that he saw fifteen men bucked and gagged in the prison; did you ever see such punishment?

Answer.—I never did, and never heard of a man being gagged there. I do not regard bucking as adding anything to the disgrace of a man who lays himself liable to be put in Castle Thunder.

Question.—How do you know that these men were guilty of any crime; inocent men are sometimes put there; were those men that were bucked found guilty of any crime?

Answer.—I do not know that they were. I have seen soldiers in the army more severely punished than at Castle thunder. Have heard of men standing on a barrel all day with the word thief written on their backs, by order of their officers. Men are often bucked in the army and tied up by the thumbs.

Question.—What is the condition of Castle Thunder?

Answer.—I believe it is very good.

Question.—You inspect the prison every morning?

Answer.—Almost every morning.

Question.—Then it would be impossible for a man to lie in his filth behind the door without you knowing it?

Answer.—It certainly would be difficult.

FREDERICK J. WILEY, sworn.

Question.—How long have you been at the Castle?

Answer.—Ever since it was established.

Question.—How long have you known me ?

Answer.—Ever since you escaped from Fort McHenry.

Question.—What is the condition of the prison.

Answer.—As clean as such a place can be kept.

Question.—What is the position of your room ?

Answer.—Where I can hear any conversation in the prisoners' room.

Question.—What language have you heard Kirby use ?

Answer.—I have heard him curse General Winder and yourself and other officials.

Question.—Did I ever do anything with him ?

Answer.—No ; although it was reported to you.

Question.—Is there a cell in the castle that a man cannot stand up erect in ?

Answer.—No, there is not.

Question.—What about the whipping ?

Answer.—I have seen eight men whipped without order of the court martial, and by order of General Winder.

Question.—How many lashes did they receive ?

Answer.—I don't think they received six lashes apiece. Some of them were Yankee deserters, and I have no doubt some of them were Confederate soldiers.

Question.—Were all these men concerned in the beating of the old man who died !

Answer.—The prisoners pointed them out, and they were their accessors.

Question.—What authority has General Winder, or anybody else, to whip a soldier on his bare back !

Answer.—I don't know, sir.

Question.—Do you know anything about prisoners being put out in the back yard ?

Answer.—Yes. They were put out there. They had fire, and some of them had blankets. It was cold weather, and the wood must have been furnished them, or they could not have got it. There were about sixty men in the yard. Captain Alexander ordered me to pick out any that were sick, and I picked out a number. The second night I picked out a number more, who were sick.

Question.—Were all these men guilty of attempting to blow up the building !

Answer.—I don't know, sir.

Question.—Is it reasonable to suppose these men would blow up the building and themselves with it.

Answer.—There are men without one redeeming trait in their characters ; would be guilty of any crime, from murder down.

Tuesday, April 28th, 1863.

The testimony for the defence was continued.

FREDERICK F. WILEY recalled.

Question.—Do you know the characters of McAlister, Shehan and Adams ?

Answer.—I was informed, some months ago, that they had made a rope to escape. Went to McAlister's cell, and asked him for it. He said he had none, and I made a search ; McAlister resisted with a spade or shovel; the other had a razor, and the other had a ball and chain. I defended myself, and drew a pistol. I found the rope in McAlister's bag. These are the characters of men we have to deal with. I would not believe McAlister on oath. One-third of the blankets distributed there, I believe, are cut up to make ropes wherewith to escape. Men are brought there sometimes with plenty of clothing and blankets, and if we are not careful they would all be stolen for the above .purpose.

Question.—What do you think of Caphart ?

Answer.—I think him one of the best officers I ever saw. If you give him an order he will carry it out. I have roomed with him, and consider him a kind hearted man. I never saw him strike a man unless he had cause.

Question.---On the night the prisoners were put into the yard, were not those who looked sick, not taken back ?

Answer.—Yes, by your order, and I helped to select them.

Question.- --Do you remember people on the street being in danger from missiles thrown from the windows ?

Answer.—Yes, and the mayor sent down word that it must be stopped'.

Question.—Did you not report the conduct of prisoners to the commanding general ?

Answer.—Yes; and he sent an order to have the guilty whipped.

Question.—Have I not always expressed solicitude for the sick ?

Answer.—Yes, you supplied many of them with clothing obtained from the battle fields around Richmond. Men are brought there very badly off for clothing.

Question.—Do you know Mr. Riggs ?

Answer.—Yes, sir, I know him.

Question.—Did you ever see him drunk ?

Answer.—Yes, very drunk, and abusive to you in your office. You said you would discharge him but for his wife and children.

Question.—Do you recollect the time Riggs went into the citizens' room ?

Answer.—I have known Riggs to be in there with the prisoners, disloyal persons, unionists, &c., up to midnight, associating with them, drinking whiskey. My room adjoins the citizens' room, and I can hear everything said.

Question.—Do yo think Captain Alexander a cruel man ?

Answer—No, sir.

Question.—How did I treat my soldiers I took down to the army ?

Answer.—Better than most of them in the army.

Question.—Was the Yankee, who was shot, running in the direction that he could escape.

Answer.—The steps he was running up lead to a porch, from whence he could have escaped. [The witness related the circumstances of the escape of the prisoner from the Libby prison, and his reception at the castle for safe keeping.] I did not know he was crazy, and was not told so. He called me to him before he died and asked my forgiveness for anything against him. [Witness related the killing of Charles Carroll *alias* Byzer, over the portico, while attempting to escape.] I believe Campbell was the cause of his death, as he got Carroll to draw the fire of the guard, so he could get out unharmed.

Question.—How long have you been at the prison?

Answer.—Since its establishment.

Question.—How many men have you seen whipped there without court martial?

Answer.—Only eight. They were whipped for beating an old man sixty years of age, from which he like to have died, and for stealing. There is no order to take the money or valuables of prisoners. If they want to give them up we take them and give them receipts. This was until recently.

Question.—What is the condition of the yard?

Answer.—It is a hard dirt floor, or clay.

Question by Captain Alexander.—It appears from the evidence that one man was tied up by the thumbs?

Answer—Yes; the only man I ever saw, and, by your order I lowered him down. His offence was stealing money and beating a negro.

Question by Capt. Alexander.—Did I not punish a man for punishing a servant without my order?

Answer.—Yes; your orders are to that effect.

Lieutenant Bossieux sworn.

Question.—Do you remember the putting of some men in the yard?

Answer.—On one instance a number were in the yard for attempting to blow up the building with powder. The first night others attempted to cut out. I staid there with the guard and caught fifteen when they came out. It was very pleasant weather. On another occasion, when some men were in the yard, there came up a storm, and I notified Mr. Ward, and they were taken in. On another occasion four Yankees were put out, and it snowed. They were taken in.

Question.—Do you think me a cruel man?

Answer.—No, sir; I do not.

Question.—Are not the doors of the cells often left open?

Answer.—Yes. I have opened them myself often.

Question by Mr. Ward.—What is your opinion of the character of the men there?

Answer.—Yes; there are some of the worst men in the world, and I don't believe there is an hour that they are not concocting some plan to escape. I dont think they could be managed with less strictness.

Question.—Do you know of a cell a man cannot stand up in?

Answer.—No, sir.

Question.—You never knew of any secret punishment?

Answer.—No, sir. The prisoners are generally brought out where all can see them.

Question.—What month was it the men were put into the yard?

Answer.—It was pleasant weather. I was out all that night without my overcoat. They staid there two days, and the third day they were taken up.

Question.—Do you know of any whipping?

Answer.—I have heard of whipping; never saw it. The whipping was by order of court martial and was laid on by the corporal of police of the castle.

Question.—Do you know any punishment not of an ordinary character?

Answer.—I recollect one circumstance. It was two men tied up to a post; don't know whether by the thumbs or the wrists. Was told it was for robbing some prisoner up stairs. Don't know how long they remained in that position.

Question by Capt. Alexander.—Do you remember me telling you once that to abstain from shooting some whose intended escape we had discovered?

Answer.—Yes.

Question by Committee.—What are your instructions in regard to prisoners putting their heads out of the windows?

Answer.—We warn them, and if they persist, the sentinels fire over them. I remember, when on Franklin street, some of the prisoners threw the sashes out of the windows, and tried to hit some of my men. They also threw bricks from the front windows. They climbed to the chimney and took bricks and threw them down.

Question by Committee.—How many men have been shot by your guard?

Answer.—None by guard. I only know of two shot there at all, the crazy Yankee, and the man Carroll. We could have shot a hundred men there, if the sentinels had been so disposed.

Question by Capt. Alexander.—Then you think if the prisoners behave themselves they will be well treated.

Answer.—Yes, I do; I know it.

GEORGE W. WAYMACK, a prisoner, sworn.

Question by Capt. Alexander.—Do you think a man put in the Castle, if he behave well, would he not be treated well?

Answer.—I do.

Question.—Did you ever see any act of cruelty there?

Answer.—I never did, sir.

Question.—When you were sick, did I not let you go home?

Answer.—You did.

Question.—When before the court martial, did I not act as your counsel?

Answer.—Yes, you did.

Question by Committee.—Where are you from?

Answer.—I am from Manchester, and am in the Castle on the charge of desertion.

Wednesday, April 29th, 1863.

JUDGE BAXTER, sworn.

Question —Judge, state what you know of the condition and treatment of prisoners.

Answer.—Captain Alexander has sent for me to examine into such cases as presented mitigating circumstances, and recommended their discharge or detention, as the case migh the. I have opportunities of seeing Captain Alexander and the prisoners. My belief is that he is peculiarly qualified to control such a body. I think his course has been one of great humanity. At his suggestion, I have discharged prisoners. There have been cases of wrong imprisonment and hardship. The management of the prison, my belief is, has been conducted with ability, and by measures of stringency required by the character of the prisoners. What was the police regulations of the cells, I don't know.

Question.—Do you know Kirby ?

Answer.—I was once at the prison for the purpose of examining into cases, and Kirby was in the room; and I requested him to leave, and he complained. Capt. Alexander had induced him so as to exclude him from the mass of prisoners.

Question by Capt. Alexander.—Judge, do you think I am a cruel man ?

Answer.—I would rather take you to be a kind man ; but firm and resolute, and not disposed to allow any of your orders to be transgressed.

Here testimony closed.

TESITMONY OF DENNIS O'CONNOR—Continued.

Prisoner is still required to report every morning at Castle Thunder upon parole. Mr. F. Wiley, an officer in Castle Thunder, cursed and abused witness this morning; charged him with being a thief. The abuse was caused by witness having been called upon to testify before the committee. Wiley has been in the habit of abusing witness. He told Wiley that he was in his power and compelled to submit to his abuse. Wiley cursed the Irish generally, and is in the habit of abusing prisoners who do not report upon their comrades. Witness is acquainted with Lieutenant Bossieux Don't know what character he bears. At one time he heard Mr. Wiley curse a prisoner who was in irons. Witness intended to join Captain Roger's company, Robinson's battalion ; denies having voted in the election for officers ;

4

never joined 19th Mississippi regiment; never was a substitute for any one.

Testimony of Captain W. N. Starke—Continued.

Witness states that he has been assigned to duty by General Winder for the purpose of investigating all cases of political, citizen and and military prisoners, and of obtaining all the necessary evidence in relation thereto. Has been in the office but a short time, and the failure to bring to trial or discharge many prisoners is attributed to the difficulty in obtaining the necessary evidence both for the prosecution and defence. Witness has been in the prison several times, and found it well regulated and cleanly.

W. N. STARKE,
Captain and Assistant Adjutant General.

Mr. Riggs' Testimony—Continued.

State what you know of Mr. Wiley's treatment of prisoners.

Answer.—It is brutal in my opinion. He cursed Webster, who was hung the other day, while Webster was in double irons. His language is brutal to prisoners, in my opinion.

Question.—Was any complaint ever made to Captain Alexander, or any report ever made in regard to Wiley's treatment of prisoners?

Answer.—I don't know.

Question.—You being there as acting assistant warden, do you not think is was your duty to report all such things?

Answer.—You told me to make reports in writing. I did not consider it my duty.

Question.—Did you not curse the guard on one occasion?

Answer.—I have no recollection of so doing.

Statements, taken under oath, and made before Robert Ward, attorney.

Statement of Lewis J. Blankenship:

Question.—How long have you been in Castle Thunder?

Answer.—I came about the 29th of July, 1862, and have been wardmaster of the hospital most of the time.

Question.—State whether you know that Kirby had a conversation with McAlister Adams and Shehan in regard to giving testimony before the congressional committee; if so, state all you know about it.

Answer.—On the day that Mr. Kirby was supœnaed to go before this committee, Mr. Shehan sent down into No. 4 room and got James McAlister out, and asked me to pass him into No. 2 hospital with Mr. Kirby, and there all three of these men consulted over the evidence which they were to give before the committee. Mr. Shehan made a statement of his evidence which he was going to testify to before the committee; wrote it out and gave it to McAlister. Mr. Shehan also wrote out Mr. Kirby's evidence and gave it to McAlister, and Macalister gave his evidence to Shehan and Kirby. Each one of the three had a written statement of the testimony which they proposed to give before the committee. The morning that Mr. Adams was summoned to go before the committee, Mr. Shehan took Mr. Adams into Mr. Kirby's room, and he and Mr. Kirby told Adams what they had testified to, and they wanted Mr. Adams to come as near as he could stating the same things before the committee, and also told him as near as they could their own testimony, and requested him to repeat the same as near as he could.

Question—Do you think there was a combination on the part of these men to injure Captain Alexander if possible ?

Answer.—I do, sir; I know that from the conversation they have had with me.

Question.—State what conversation you allude to.

Answer.—I have heard Mr. Shehan say that Captain Alexander was nothing but a God damned loafer ; that he intended to get him out of here if he possibly could ; that nobody suited this place but Mr. Riggs, and that if Mr. Riggs were captain of this prison he could get out whenever he pleased ; that Captain Alexander was not fit to have command of a parcel of hogs. Long before this committee was appointed I have heard McAlister say that Captain Alexander had done all he could to have him shot, and that if he ever had it in his power he would have his revenge out of him. About two days before he was summoned he said every dog had his day and that his day had just come. Mr. Kirby, Mr. Shehan, and McAlister all knew that the committee was going to enter into the examination of Castle Thunder, and the three wrote a letter to Mr. Riggs about the committee before it was appointed, and after Mr. Riggs had been discharged from Castle Thunder. I don't know that Mr. Riggs ever got the letter, but I am confident the letter went out of the building by private hands. That letter stated that a committee was going to be appointed to examine into things here at Castle Thunder, and they wished him to lay the letter before Congress, and if he did not like to do it himself to give it to Mr. Blanc, the hospital steward.

Question.—State what was the character of these men.

Answer.—In regard to McAlister, I staid in No. 4 room with him for about four weeks, and during the time I was in the room, I don't think a night passed that some robbery of clothes, hats, shoes, or money was not committed by some one in the adjacent large room, and handed to McAlister through a crack or hole which he had cut through the partition which separated the two rooms, and received by him and sold by him whenever he got opportunity to sell. Frequently these stolen things were handed to McAlister through the crack by Shehan who was then on his parole, and acting as corporal of the police about the building. I don't know anything dishonest about Mr. Kirby, but I know of Mr. Adams having stolen a pair of boots, and selling them to McAlister, and also he stole four sheets out of the hospitals which I found in his knapsack. He also stole a blanket from the hospital which I also found in his possession.

Question.—What is the conduct of the men *generally* who have been in Castle Thunder?

Answer.—The largest proportion of the men are real rascals; guilty of cutting the building for the purpose of escaping, fighting, abusing each other, committing robberies and bribery of sentinels.

Question.—Have you seen any punishments inflicted in this prison?

Answer.—None, sir, but what I thought were well deserved. I saw a man of Wheat's battalion whipped for desertion by sentence of court martial. I heard Captain Alexander tell him he was sorry to have it to do but he was obliged to do it. Samuel Lebrick, the name of the man who was whipped, shook hands with the corporal of the police, and asked him for a drink of whiskey, which was given him by order of Captain Alexander. He was whipped very lightly.

Statement of J. B. Evans.

Question.—How long have you been in Castle Thunder?

Answer.—I have been here about ten weeks.

Question.—Do you know of any combination among the prisoners to injure the reputation of Captain Alexander in any manner? If so, please state it.

Answer.—I saw Shehan, Adams and McAlister before they went before the committee, go to Mr. Kirby, and they asked him what they should say before the committee. I have heard McAlister and Adams both say that they would swear to anything to injure the Captain. Adams said that if he had one more chance to go before the committee he would swear that Captain Alexander was always drunk.

Question.—What is the character of these men?

Answer.—They are of a desperate character. Adams told me he had been in the penitentiary twice. I have heard Shehan say that he has received money from prisoners to get them out when he was corporal of the police, and I heard Adams say that he had taken fifty dollars from Captain Callan. I heard McAlister send word to Kirby to have him summoned, that he would like to have a chance to swear against the Captain; he would do all he could to injure him.

Question.—Do you know whether Mr. Kirby ever sent out letters privately from the building?

Answer.—Yes, I have seen him send them out and receive them through private sources.

STATE OF VIRGINIA, }
  City of Richmond, } *to-wit :*

I, Robert D. Ward, do certify that the foregoing statements made
by Lewis J. Blankenship and J. B. Evans, were sworn to by them
respectively, before me. Given under my hand this 28th day of April,
1863.

R. D. WARD, N. P.

WALKER'S ARTILLERY BATTALION, }
'Camp Maury, near Milford, April 26, 1863. }

DEAR CAPTAIN : The summons of Hon. C. C. Herbert, directing
me to appear before the special committee of Congress, on the 23d
inst., did not reach me until yesterday the 25th inst. I immediately
applied for leave of absence to enable me to obey the summons, but
found that no officer of the army will be allowed to take the cars, except upon the special order of General Lee.

My application for two days leave (enclosing the summons) has
been forwarded through the regular channels to General Lee, and it
will be over a week before it can be heard from. I fear that the de-
liberations of the committee will be closed before I can obtain permis-
sion to leave camp.

If you think it important for me to appear before the committee
without delay, you might procure an order from the Secretary of
War, directing my immediate appearance.

If the committee anticipates remaining in session over a week,
please advise me of the fact and I will go down as soon as General
Lee's permit is received.

I assure you it will afford me pleasure to bear testimony to the
systematic and able manner in which you have managed the provost
prison under your charge, and to the humanity and kindness with
which you have treated the prisoners in your custody.

You have the greatest talent for controlling and managing desperate characters, and I have often said that I do not believe that
there is another man in the Southern Confederacy who can fill your
present position.

Hoping that the report of the committee will triumphantly vindicate you, (as it will do) from the malicious charges which have been
preferred against you,

I remain your friend,
GREENLEE DAVIDSON.

HEADQUARTERS, DEPARTMENT OF HENRICO, }
Richmond, April 28, 1863. }

Captain ALEXANDER,

SIR: In reply to your communication, I state that, in consequence of the violent proceedings of the prisoners in blowing up the building, garroting and using slung shot upon the newly arrived prisoners, robbing and endangering their lives, I gave you orders to punish these ruffians severely, and if necessary, to resort to coporeal punishment.

Respectfully,

JNO. H. WINDER, *Brigadier General.*

CAPTAIN ALEXANDER'S DEFENCE.

CASTLE THUNDER, Richmond, April 13, 1863.

To the Honorable Committee of the House of Representatives, C. S. A.,
for the investigation of Castle Thunder:

GENTLEMEN: Bonaparte said: " That the first requisite in an officer
was health, the second temper; without the first the second is seldom
found, and without the second, a good officer, mingling the gentleman
with the commander, cannot exist."

> " The elephant is never won with anger,
> Nor should the man who would reclaim the lion
> Take him by the teeth."

There is nothing so degrading to an officer of rank as an intemperate reprimand, and before his inferiors. If he be respectful, as he
would have others respect him, *and forgets not that he is a gentleman*, his
conduct is said to have merited the rebuke from his not having defended
it. If both parties loose their temper, a court martial follows, and
neither party gains by the result. To make a good officer, a man
must be a gentleman, and they are inseparable. The man who cannot
command his tongue, is the worst man to entrust with any command.
The supercilious and the arrogant, always meet from men endowed
with common sense the contempt such frivolity deserves.

So much for my opinion of a man placed at the head of any public
affair. Now, I will proceed to state, in as concise a manner as possible, my views, which I respectfully submit to your honorable notice.
This subject I feel I cannot handle, although fraught with some interest
to you, and much anxiety to me. When this cruel war was forced
upon us, on the secession of Virginia I was among the first to resign
from the old navy, and take up arms. I chose the army, and shoul-
dering my musket, enrolled myself as a private. My career and
advancement since then is known. I followed my unfortunate leader
far within the enemy's lines, *never questioning an order*, but obeyed all;
never asking, where go we? We fell. I suffered; but thank God escaped
from the tyranny of the " usurper of rights," and have tried to deal
them some good blows. My injuries placed me in command of this
post. Here, I have tried to do my duty, and no matter what may be
said or done, you cannot keep this strong right arm idle; it shall work,
either as an officer or private, until we achieve what we are all strug-
gling for—the vindication of a sacred right; self-government. I
trust I have clearly demonstrated to this honorable body the character

of the men who have been committed to my care—the murderer, the
robber, the deserter, the substitute deserter, the pickpocket, and worst
of all, the skulker; the man who by his skulking endangers his comrades; therefore, worse than the murderer. The spy, the reconstruc-
tionist, the disloyal; all, all that are inimical to our glorious cause
are thrust upon me. Why? Because this Castle is the only penitentiary
the Confederacy has. I have proved that rules and regulations were
regularly distributed; that they were repeatedly told that punishment
would follow a persistency in wrong doing. That the place only
acquired a bad name by the conduct of the fiends that inhabited it;
and that punishment were only resorted to when it became absolutely
necessary, and it had become unsafe for a man to enter the wards. I
have proved that while our noble army was in the field subsisting on
corn, these fiends were being fed on full rations, and then would refuse
positively to rejoin their suffering comrades, and could only be forced
there at the point of the bayonet.

That some men were whipped on the back, is true. *Does it appear in
the voluminous evidence that* there was a single man, not by the order of
a court martial, or one from a State represented by any representa-
tive in our legislative halls. It was represented by one of the
witnesses, that men were tied up by the thumbs and gagged. The
witness, who, by the way, was proven to have been discharged from
his place for "moral incapacity," is certainly mistaken, or saw it in
one of his drunken dreams, for it does not appear in the evidence,
and I say it is not so. In fact, I think that if those horrid brutalities
existed, the witnesses, or whoever made the statement, were very
culpable to report them only when they were turned disgracefully
away from this place. A man who knows a wrong to exist and reports it not, is more guilty than the wrong doer. I might here state
that evidence also shows that when the hordes of the invader threatened close our walls, I did not rest safe within, but threw myself into
the breach, and when the smoke of battle receded, and we were again
free from their accursed presence, I turned my attention to the care
of those brave men who shed their blood in our defence, and who,
maimed, were bourne to my doors. Many remember the little hospital
of the "Angel of Mercy," where thirty beds were always kept, and
the brave were cared for by a pale, little Virginia woman—my wife.
Do the records show the loss of a single limb or life from that hospital, or do they show a single bill paid by the Confederate States
government, for its support? I do not like, gentlemen, to recount
these things, but I am a stranger to you, and I would rather you
would condemn me to be shot than to promulgate, upon such evidence
as you have had before you—from your legislative halls—that I am
cruel. There are men in your honorable body, who know me and
know my career. All men conversant with military law, know that
if a man persists in passing a sentry without the countersign, he risks
his life. That two men have been shot here, is also true; one, an
Irishman, who substituted for a gentleman from Halifax, and the same
night deserted, while in sight of the enemy; afterwards captured,
locked up here, and persisting in an attempt to escape, was killed.

Another, a Yankee, who, rushing past the sentry, attempted to fly by the back entrance—killed—they say he was crazy. The sentry did not know it; nor I, or I might, for I believe one half of them are crazy.

I have demonstrated here before this honorable committee that some characters that have been committed here to my charge have been without a redeeming point. I have appealed in every way to them, until at last endurance was worn out, and corporeal punishment did much good. Does it appear from the evidence that Southern volunteers were ever struck except by officer Causey in self defence? The committee have been made aware of the immense number of prisoners I have handled—*thousands*—and yet it appears that only about twenty have been punished. Does that look cruel?

Are not soldiers in camp when guilty of little peccadilloes bucked and made to ride a cannon or a wooden horse? These fiends are only bucked; is that in comparison cruel? This being a receptacle for all that is bad, would I not have been justifiable had I been present when that master-fiend, Webster, who expiated his crimes on the gallows, contemplated murder, and attempted to escape, to have shot him or ordered my guard to do so.

Have I not proven, by the very prisoners themselves, whom I have taken *ad libitum*, that the character of many of the prisoners is terrible, and that I have been lenient? Have I not proven that I have done many acts of kindness and charity, yea, many, far outnumbering the alleged cruelties? Have I not proven that the only witnesses who seem to think I have been in the least cruel, knew of these things before, and only reported them when they had been sent away from the prison, as being no farther of any use? Have I not proven my vigilance and strict adherence to right, and my energy in carrying out all orders of my superiors? Have I not proven my economy and personal supervision to prevent extravagance or waste of all government stores committed to my charge? Have I not proven that by my own individual exertions, I have clothed many prisoners who were being sent to the field? When, as some of the witnesses say, were men exposed to the weather? Have I not proven their infernal character, and were not their comrades at that time, whom they had shamefully deserted, fighting our battles, and sleeping on the cold ground, without tent or other cover than the canopy of heaven.

I would here say a few words about the witnesses examined. Mr. Bland, a hospital steward, whom it appears, from the evidence, was a man not fit to be about a public institution, his depravity was such that he was disgracefully ordered away. He says he was five months in a Yankee prison and saw better treatment. I rather think that that argues badly for Mr. Bland, for while I was a prisoner among that hateful people, the only one I saw treated well was one who, sycophant-like, courted favor at their hands. I was kept in a cell seven by four for three weeks, that cell under ground and no window; moreover, prisoners of war are entitled to better treatment than murderers, deserters, spys, &c.

Witness No. 2, Kirby, the spy. I hardly think it fair to take prisoners' evidence; but I waive that and challenge the whole prison. His evidence shows that although he is incarcerated as that most hateful of all things, a spy; yet he is put in the best room in the Castle, has a fire, good bed and is allowed to purchase anything from the outside that he may require. Oh! gentlemen, does this look cruel? And then he is only removed from this room when the true instincts of the beast were developed and he proves to be a low-born blackguard.

Witness No. 3. One Adams, who served out a term in the penitentiary, was pardoned during a second term, and deserted in sight of the enemy.

Witness No. 4. A man who will not tell where he is from, and is sentenced to three years imprisonment.

Witness No. 5. Shehan, a deserter, a man who has broken his parole, and since he has given in his evidence has again deserted his comrades. One or two others close the list, and the least said about them the better.

Gentlemen, I leave the matter in your hands, well satisfied the action you take will be just action. I stand before the people and press of this country, and invite at any time the strictest investigation.

· I am, respectfully, your obedient servant,

G. W. ALEXANDER.

A. A. G. and A. P. M. commanding Castle Thunder.

www.ingramcontent.com/pod-product-compliance
Lightning Source LLC
Chambersburg PA
CBHW031751090426
42739CB00008B/969